A Cross-Cultural Study of Consumer Attitudes and Emotional Responses of Apparel Purchase Behavior

王韻　著

封面設計：實踐大學教務處出版組

出 版 心 語

　　近年來，全球數位出版蓄勢待發，美國從事數位出版的業者超過百家，亞洲數位出版的新勢力也正在起飛，諸如日本、中國大陸都方興未艾，而台灣卻被視為數位出版的處女地，有極大的開發拓展空間。植基於此，本組自民國 93 年 9 月起，即醞釀規劃以數位出版模式，協助本校專任教師致力於學術出版，以激勵本校研究風氣，提昇教學品質及學術水準。

　　在規劃初期，調查得知秀威資訊科技股份有限公司是採行數位印刷模式並做數位少量隨需出版〔POD＝Print on Demand〕（含編印銷售發行）的科技公司，亦為中華民國政府出版品正式授權的 POD 數位處理中心，尤其該公司可提供「免費學術出版」形式，相當符合本組推展數位出版的立意。隨即與秀威公司密集接洽，出版部李協理坤城數度親至本組開會討論，雙方就數位出版服務要點、數位出版申請作業流程、出版發行合約書以及出版合作備忘錄等相關事宜逐一審慎研擬，歷時 9 個月，至民國 94 年 6 月始告順利簽核公布。

這段期間，承蒙本校謝前校長孟雄、謝副校長宗興、王教務長又鵬、藍教授秀璋以及秀威公司宋總經理政坤等多位長官給予本組全力的支持與指導，本校多位教師亦不時從旁鼓勵與祝福，在此一併致上最誠摯的謝意。本校新任校長張博士光正甫上任（民國 94 年 8 月），獲知本組推出全國大專院校首創的數位出版服務，深表肯定與期許。諸般溫馨滿溢，將是挹注本組持續推展數位出版的最大動力。

本出版團隊由葉立誠組長、王雯珊老師、賴怡勳老師三人為組合，以極其有限的人力，充分發揮高效能的團隊精神，合作無間，各司統籌策劃、協商研擬、視覺設計等職掌，在精益求精的前提下，至望弘揚本校實踐大學的校譽，具體落實出版機能。

實踐大學教務處出版組　謹識

中華民國 96 年 4 月

Table of contents

List of figures

List of tables

Chapter 1
Introduction

Consumers are likely to form many different judgments while viewing commercials or evaluating products and services. These judgments eventually will turn into attitudes consumer holds toward the object and result in the consumer's purchase behavior (Fishbein, 1963). From an early presentation by Rosenberg and Hovland (1960), three components of attitudes were introduced - affect (emotion), cognition (knowledge) and conation (action). Several studies have provided support for the interrelated nature of these affective, cognitive and conative attitudinal components (Ajzen & Fishbein, 1980; Breckler & Wiggins, 1989; Hilgard, 1980; Miniard & Barone, 1997). Moreover, attitude is a result of learning and is strongly influenced by personal experience, family and friends and marketing (Eagly & Chaiken, 1993). Some researches include additional variables in their models for consumer purchase behavior such as social factors, situational or personal control, and advertising and brand attitude (Ajzen & Madden, 1986; Bagozzi & Warshaw, 1990; Edell & Burke, 1987; Ajzen & Fishbein, 1980; Triandis, 1977).

The most frequently used theory related to attitude research is the Theory of Reasoned Action (TRA) (Sheppard, Hartwick, & Warshaw, 1988). The Theory of Reasoned Action (TRA) (Fishbein & Ajzen, 1975) includes two parts: (1) the attitude toward the object- including beliefs and the evaluation of object, and (2) subjective norms which influence consumers' intention. According to the Theory of Reasoned Action (TRA), behavior is predictable from the consumer's intention, and the consumer intention will be influenced by consumer attitude toward the object and the consumer's subjective norms, which are consumers' responses to social factors. Triandis (1977) offered a competing multi-attribute model of the attitude-intention-behavior relationship which views behavior as determined by intention, habit and facilitating conditions with the intention being formatted by affects, cognition and social factors. The TRA and Triandis models, which are often called the theory of consumer purchase intention in consumer behavior, will be used as the theoretical background model in this study.

Recent theories and debates have challenged the Theory of Reasoned Action's assumption that attitudes are mediated by belief, arguing that attitudes are instead mediated by emotions (Härtel, McColl-Kennedy, & McDonald, 1998; Herr, 1995; Miniard & Barone, 1997; Weiner, 1995; Weiss & Cropanzano, 1996). Current models of persuasion (Lutz, 1990; Mitchell & Olson, 1981; Petty & Cacioppo, 1986) assume that attitude formation and change are based on the acquisition and retrieval of verbal information about the product, and individuals translate the visual and emotional elements of advertisements into verbal product-related information. In addition, in a robust research study using 23,000 respondents with 240 advertisements in different product categories, Morris, Woo, Geason, and Kim (2002) found affect (emotion) dominates over cognition (knowledge) for predicting conative attitude (action). Recently, studies investigating affective responses have increased (Aaker, Stayman, & Vezina, 1988; Edell & Burke, 1987; Holbrook & Batra, 1987; Morris, Woo, Geason, & Kim, 2002; Sunil, 1998). Throughout the relevant theory and research literature, the terms "affect," "emotion," and "mood" are frequently used interchangeably (Batson, Shaw, & Oleson, 1992; Cohen & Areni, 1991; Derbaix & Pham, 1998).

Although researchers have studied aspects of emotions created and manipulated by advertisements in general (Aaker et al., 1988; Edell & Burke, 1987; Holbrook & Batra, 1987; Morris et al., 2002), little research can be found that focuses on the effect that cultural differences have on processing these types of messages (Callow & Schiffman, 2002). This study proposes to address this deficit in the literature. The emerging markets in Asia are increasingly affluent, and success in these countries is a priority for multinational corporations. The influence of culture is particularly important in transferring marketing strategy across borders, because communication patterns are closely linked to cultural norms (Hong, Muderrisoglu, & Zinkhan, 1987). Cross-cultural research studies allow for the verification of universality of theory application or for the expansion of theory (Lee & Green, 1991; Malhotra & McCort, 2001). Americans and Chinese exhibit major differences with respect to cultural dimensions of collectivism-individualism; that is, the extent to which an individual considers the requirements of the relevant group, as opposed to his or her individual requirements in making decisions (Bond, Leung, & Wan, 1982; Hofstede, 2001).

Taiwan is an island about 160 kilometers off the southeast coast of mainland China with a size of 14,000 square miles and a population of 22.5 million. The national income reached $265,624 million in 1999 with an economic growth rate of 5.42% (Statistical Yearbook of The Republic of China, 2003). The Taiwan market may seem small but it has a steady economic growth rate, and strong consumer demand. According to the United States Department of Commerce (2001), Taiwan is eighth in total U.S. trade (imports and exports), which reached $51.5 million in 2001. In fact, exports of goods and services from the United States to Taiwan have increased from \$4.7 billion in 1985 to \$24.38 billion in 2000 (United States Department of Commerce, 2001).

Since consumer attitude, social influence and individual differences have been found to be important predictors for consumer purchase behavior, firms wanting to increase sales in apparel retailing should try to understand consumers' attitudes toward shopping apparel, their emotional responses in the shopping environment, subjective norms which influence social factors, and the individual differences such as fashion involvement, the need for cognition and emotion. This research investigated the role of consumers' emotional responses, attitudes toward apparel shopping, subjective norms and individual differences in influencing consumers' apparel purchase intention in cross-cultural marketing. Questions this research sought to answer were: Do emotional responses influence consumer purchase behavior in the apparel-shopping environment? Does fashion involvement have an influence on apparel purchases? Does an individual's difference in the need for cognition have an influence on apparel purchase behavior? Will the different cultural dimensions result in differences in subjective norms for consumer intention to purchase apparel?

Statement of Purpose

The purpose of this study was to examine the roles of consumers' emotional responses, attitudes toward apparel shopping, subjective norms in social influence, individual differences and demographic factors for Taiwan and U.S. consumers' apparel purchase intentions and their actual purchase behavior. The study is organized into four objectives in the following section.

First Objective

The first objective was to investigate the relationships among apparel purchase behavior, apparel purchase intention and the variables of apparel purchase antecedents such as consumers' attitude toward shopping apparel, emotional responses, and social factors for U.S. and Taiwanese consumers. After reviewing the two major theories in consumer purchase behavior, the main difference between the Theory of Reasoned Action (TRA) and the Triandis model is the emotional component. According to Al-khaldiand Wallace (1999) and Karahanna and Straub (1999), the measures of consequence of attitude and social factors in the Triandis model were identical to the Theory of Reasoned Action's attitude toward object and subjective norms. With the additional construct, emotion, in the Triandis Model, it is hypothesized that the Triandis Model will be able to predict consumer apparel purchase intention more accurately than the TRA model. Therefore, the following hypothesis is proposed.

Hypothesis 1a: The emotional responses while shopping for apparel will have an effect on their apparel purchase intention.

Previous research has suggested that the physical environment of malls is an important determinant of consumers' behavioral responses (e.g., Bellenger et al., 1980; Finn, McQuityy, and Rigby, 1994; McGoldrick & Thompson, 1992). The physical environment includes elements such as layout, interior architecture and décor, lighting, music, aromas and cleanliness (Baker, 1986). Several store-level studies have examined the effect of a single environmental element, such as music (Dube, Chebat, & Morin, 1995), color (Crowley, 1993) and scent (Spangenberg, Crowley, and Henderson, 1996). In addition, Akhter, Andrews, and Durvasula (1994) and Donovan, Rossiter, Marcoolyn, and Nesdale (1994) found that general perceptions of the store or mall interior influence the approach and time spent in the environment and amount of sales.

Hypothesis 1b: The attitudes of consumers toward apparel shopping will have a positive effect on consumer' apparel purchase intention.

Several research studies support the linkage between the physical environment and emotional responses. Baker et al. (1992) established the links between store environment, the affective states of pleasure and arousal, and behavioral intentions. Darden and Babin (1994) found that consumers' emotions are associated with retail environments and strongly related to a store's tangible characteristics.

Hypothesis 1c: Apparel shopping attitude factors of store ambience and services will have significant correlations to consumers' emotional responses.

In consumer behavior theories, both the TRA and the Triandis model included social factors in predicting consumer purchase behavior. A reference group, which is a part of social factors, is an actual or imaginary individual or group conceived of having significant relevance upon an individual's evaluations, aspirations, or behavior (Park & Lessig, 1977). According to Sillars (1995), parents and other family members serve as channels of information, sources of social pressure, and support for one another; this family norm creates a distinct lifestyle, pattern of decision-making, and style of interacting. Children, accepting this distinct family lifestyle as the norm, have continuous opportunities to learn and internalize the beliefs, attitudes, and values they have observed (Sears, 1983). Furthermore, Heckler et al. (1989) found purchase similarities and observed stronger impacts in parent-child intergenerational influences for convenience goods than for shopping goods. The behavioral intentions approach used in the current research traditionally has termed this concept, the subjective norm. Subjective norms are the consumer's overall perceptions of what relevant individuals think he or she should do (Ryan,

1982). Conceptual and empirical work appears to support the importance of social referents as a factor in determining shopping behavior or clothing purchase behavior (Ajzen & Fishbein, 1980). Therefore, the following hypothesis is proposed:

Hypothesis 1d: The subjective norm will have a positive effect on the apparel purchase intention of consumers.

Regarding the relationship between the consumer intention and consumer purchase behavior, three social psychology studies (Ajzen, 1985; Ajzen & Fishbein, 1980; Darroch, 1971) have provided evidence indicating the need to include intention as a moderator variable even though situational variables were controlled. The relationship between purchase behavior and behavioral intentions has been found contingent on the time interval (Wilson, 1975). When intention and behavior measures were contiguous or nearly contiguous, correlations between intention and behavior were high. The Theory of Reasoned Action model seldom distinguishes between intention and behavior. However, in this research, both consumers' purchase intention and the purchase behavior were measured, and then the relationship among antecedent factors and purchase behavior was examined. According to previous findings, we have the following hypothesis:

Hypothesis 1e: Consumer purchase intention will have a mediating effect on their apparel purchase behavior and the variables of purchase antecedents such as consumers' attitude toward shopping apparel, emotional responses, and subjective norms.

Second Objective

The second objective was to examine whether U.S. and Taiwan consumers exhibit any cultural difference in their apparel purchase antecedents and apparel purchase behavior. According to Triandis (1995) perhaps the most important dimension of cultural difference is individualism and collectivism. Triandis (1995) stated that members of individualist cultures (the United States) tend to hold an independent view of the self that emphasizes separateness, internal attributes, and the uniqueness of individuals. In contrast, members of collectivist cultures (Taiwan) tend to hold an interdependent view of the self that emphasized connectedness, social context, and relationships.

It can be explained that people in the collectivistic culture are more concerned with others' reactions and the significance of personal relationships than people in individualistic cultures (Yang, 1992). In addition, people in collectivist cultures are more conservative. This difference suggests that consumer behavior may be different in Taiwan and United States. Therefore, the following hypotheses were proposed:

Hypothesis 2a: The subjective norm will have more influence on purchase intention of Taiwan consumers which are collectivist than on purchase intention of U.S. consumers which are individualist.

Hypothesis 2b: Consumer attitudes toward apparel shopping will have more influence on purchase intention of Taiwan consumers which are collectivist than on purchase intention of U.S. consumers which are individualist.

Hypothesis 2c: Consumer emotional responses while shopping will have more influence on purchase intention of U.S. consumers which are individualist than on purchase intention of Taiwan consumers which are collectivist.

Third Objective

In addition to consumers' emotional responses, attitude toward apparel shopping attributes, and subjective norms, the third objective was to examine the moderating effect of individual differences in the need for cognition, the need for emotion and apparel involvement on their apparel purchase intention. The need for cognition represents the tendency for individuals to engage in and enjoy thinking (Cacioppo & Petty, 1982). The need for emotion is defined as "the tendency or propensity for individuals to seek out emotional situations, enjoy emotional stimuli, and exhibit a preference to use emotion in interacting with the world" (Raman, Chattopadhyay, & Hoyer, 1995, p. 537). An individual who has a high need for cognition is more likely to organize, elaborate, and evaluate the detail for apparel shopping attributes to which he/she is exposed, since he/she has a need to structure situations in meaningful ways. On the other hand, individuals who have a high need for emotion are more likely to counter the stores' atmospheres and generate the purchase intention based on their sensory experiences. Therefore, the following hypotheses were purposed:

Hypothesis 3a: The need for cognition of consumers will have a moderating effect on their apparel purchase intention and apparel purchase antecedents such as attitude toward shopping apparel, emotional responses, and subjective norms.

Hypothesis 3b: The need for emotion of consumers will have a moderating effect on their apparel purchase intention and apparel purchase antecedents such as attitude toward shopping apparel, emotional responses, and subjective norms.

Involvement is the heart of the person-object relationship and the relational variable is most predictive of purchase behavior (Evrard & Aurier, 1996; Martin, 1998). Involvement has been discussed and utilized to examine fashion clothing in a number of prior studies (Browne & Kaldenberg, 1997; Fairhurst, Good, & Gentry, 1989; Flynn & Goldsmith, 1993; Tigert, Ring, & King, 1976). The highly fashion involved consumer has historically been important to fashion researchers and marketers, because they are seen as the drivers, influentials and legitimists of the fashion adoption process (Goldsmith, Moore, & Beaudoin, 1999; Tigert et al., 1976). The nature and role of fashion clothing and its function for individuals have also been shown to result in major differences in fashion involvement across cultures (Tigert, King, & Ring, 1980).

> Hypothesis 3c: The level of consumers' apparel involvement will have a moderating effect on their apparel purchase intention and apparel purchase antecedents such as attitude toward shopping apparel, emotional responses, and social factors.

Fourth Objective

In addition to consumers' attitude toward apparel shopping, consumers' emotional responses, social factors, cultural and individual differences, the fourth objective is to examine the demographic factors of age, gender, occupation, income, and education level.

Hypothesis 4: The demographic variables of consumers in U.S. and Taiwan will be related to their attitude toward apparel shopping, emotional responses, subjective norms, apparel purchase intention and apparel behavior.

Limitations

Data were collected in Taiwan and U.S. to represent Eastern and Western cultures. However, there are many countries in the East and West that might have different perspectives from Taiwan and U.S. consumers. Additionally, this study only examines the product category in consumers' apparel purchase intention related to consumers' emotional response, apparel shopping attributes, subjective norms, personal differences in the need for cognition, emotional, and fashion involvement constructs. Other product categories should use the results of this study with caution. Also, there are some constructs that may have influence on consumers' apparel purchase behavior which are not included in this study. For instance, the situational factors for out-of-stock merchandise, time pressure, and consumer subjective knowledge in clothing may influence consumers' purchase behavior. Generally, the results generated from this study should be interpreted carefully with consideration of these limitations.

Concept and Definitions

The following terms and definitions are presented for clarification of the text:

Consumer behavior: "... the study of human responses to products, services, and the marketing of products and services" (Kardes, 2001, p. 5).

Clothing behavior: "... interest in clothing, attitudes toward clothing, use of clothing, purchase of clothing, and possession and accumulation of clothing" (Hoffman, 1970, p. 296).

Intention: "... a psychological construct distinct from attitude represents the person's motivation in the sense of his or her conscious plan to exert effort to carry out a behavior" (Eagly & Chaiken, 1993, p. 168).

Cognitive component of attitude: "… the knowledge and perceptions that are acquired by a combination of direct experience with the attitude object and related information from various sources" (Schiffman & Kanuk, 2004, p.202).

Affect: Affect is understood to be the most general term, implying a global state. In addition, emotion and mood are conceptualized as substates of affect (Batson et al., 1992). Affect may be seated in the midbrain, informing the individual as to "… those states of affairs that is valued more than others. Change from a less valued to a more valued state is accompanied by positive affect…. Intensity of the affect reveals the magnitude of the value preference" (Baston et al., 1992, p.298).

Emotion: "… emotion is most directly related to goal-driven behavior, especially the possibility of obtaining a goal of interest and a perceived change in the individual's relationship to that goal" (Baston et al., 1992, p. 300). Schwarz and Clore (1988) made a distinction between moods and emotions. Moods are general positive or negative feelings that people have at a particular time (e.g., being in a good or bad mood). In contrast, emotions such as anger and jealousy are more distinctive in tone and have an identifiable cause.

Conation: "… the action a person wants to take toward the object" (Sheth, Mittal, & Newman, 1999, p. 391).

Attitude: "Attitude is a psychological tendency that is expressed by evaluating a particular entity with some degree of favor or disfavor" (Eagly & Chaiken, 1993, p.1).

Belief: In the Theory of Reasoned Action, the b_i is the behavioral belief that performing the behavior leads to some consequence "i" (i.e., subjective probability that the behavior has the consequence "i") (Ajzen & Fishbein, 1980).

Evaluation: In the Theory of Reasoned Action, the e*i* is the evaluation of consequence *i* (Ajzen & Fishbein, 1980).

Subjective norm (SN): is a function of the normative beliefs (NB) and motivations to comply (MC) with those beliefs (Ajzen & Fishbein, 1980).

Normative belief (NB): is the respondent's belief that referent approves or does not approve of the behavior (Ajzen & Fishbein, 1980).

Motivations to comply (MC): is the respondent's willingness to comply with referent (Ajzen & Fishbein, 1980).

Reference group: is "an actual or imaginary individual or group conceived of having significant relevance upon an individual's evaluations, aspiration, or behavior" (Park & Lessig, 1977, p 102).

Cultural: "… the interactive aggregate of common characteristics that influences a group's response to its environment" (Hofstede, 2001, p. 19).

The need for cognition: represents the tendency for individuals to engage in and enjoy thinking (Cacioppo & Petty, 1982).

The need for emotion: is defined as "the tendency or propensity for individuals to seek out emotional situations, enjoy emotional stimuli, and exhibit a preference to use emotion in interacting with the world" (Raman, Chattopadhyay, & Hoyer, 1995, p. 537).

Involvement: is defined as "a person's perceived relevance of the object based on their inherent needs, values, and interests" (Zaichkowsky, 1985, p. 341).

Operational Definitions

Attitude: In the Theory of Reasoned Action the estimation of the attitude was calculated by multiply these two components (1) strength of the beliefs (b) about this behavior, and (2) the individual's subjective evaluation of those beliefs (e) (Ajzen & Fishbein, 1980). For instance, the overall attitude toward the apparel purchase behavior was calculated by the multiplication of the evaluation score (e i) and the belief score (b i), and by summing across the apparel shopping attributes.

Belief: perceived consequences in consumer attitude toward the object's attribute performance, the object can be product or service; beliefs that the product contains each attribute are measured using a seven-point "likely-unlikely" scale; asking the respondent the likelihood that each outcome was rated in each attribute (Ajzen & Fishbein, 1980). For instance, with 7 being "very likely" and 1 being "very unlikely" consumers are asked to indicate how likely they think it is that apparel possesses each of the apparel shopping attributes.

Evaluation: Consumer's evaluation of perceived consequences in each attribute's importance; the evaluations of each outcome were measured on seven-point scale by asking how "important-unimportant" the outcome was to the consumer (Ajzen & Fishbein, 1980). For instance, with 7 being "very important" and 1 being "very unimportant" consumers are asked to indicate how important they consider of these apparel-shopping attributes when they purchase apparel.

Subjective norms: In the Theory of Reasoned Action the estimation of the subjective norm is a function of these two components (1) Normative beliefs which is the person's belief that the salient referent thinks he/she should (or should not) perform the behavior, and (2) his/her motivations to comply to that referent. The summation of outcomes of normative beliefs multiplied by motivation to comply represents subjective norm (Ajzen & Fishbein, 1980).

Normative beliefs (NB): Respondents indicated their normative beliefs with regard to each referent by responding to questions such as: "Do your family members support your apparel purchase behavior?" Respondents' answers will be measured on a 5-point scale ranging from 1 (*not at all*) to 5 (*strongly support*).

Motivations to comply (MC): Motivation to comply is measured by using the same referents in the NB by answering questions such as: "How often do your family members' opinions influence your apparel purchase decision?" on a 5-point scale, from 1 (*not at all*) to 5 (*very often*). Both normative beliefs and motivation to comply scales are unipolar scales, since people are unlikely to be motivated to do the opposite of what their salient referents think they should do (cf. Ajzen & Fishbein, 1980, p. 75).

Intention scale: Four items of a 5-point semantic differential scale were used to measure consumers' apparel purchase intention. Compared to Ajzen and Fishbein (1980) measurement scale, which only has one item to measure intention, this 4-item scale will have better reliability. Consumers were asked to indicate their apparel purchase intention for today's shopping by the following items: "unlikely/likely, impossible/possible, improbable/probable, and uncertain/certain to buy." This scale has been used by Oliver and Bearden (1985), Shimp and Sharma (1987), and Yi (1990), and has shown consistently high reliability. In addition to this scale, two items that independently measure consumer intention were included: (1) consumers' beliefs regarding their purchase intention for apparel today and (2) consumers' opinions of the goal for today's shopping trip, whether browsing, buying a specific item, or both.

Emotional scale: The Richins's (1997) Consumption Emotion Set (CES), a 17-items scale, was used to measure consumers' emotional responses after their purchase behavior. Respondents were asked to indicate their feeling on a five-point scale from 1 (*not at all*) to 5 (*very strongly*) to express how strongly they felt about each of the emotional responses, e.g., anger, joy, and love.

Individual difference in the need for cognition (NFC): Cacioppo and Petty (1982) developed a 34-items NFC measurement scale that had high internal consistency reliability (.91). Later, Cacioppo, Petty, & Chuan (1984) developed the short form of NFC measurement scale, which only contained 18 items and has high internal reliability (α = .90). Respondents indicated their agreement to the need for cognition phrase from 1 (*strongly disagree*) to 5 (*strongly agree*). For instance, one item asked respondents to indicate how they thought about themselves, "I would prefer complex rather than simple problems." Higher scores mean consumers have a higher need for cognition.

Individual difference in the need for emotion (NFE): The NFE scale was developed by Raman, Chattopadhyay, and Hoyer (1995), which is composed of 12 items scored on a five-point Likert-type scale ranging from 1 (*strongly disagree*) to 5 (*strongly agree*). For instance, respondents indicated their disagreement /agreement with "experiencing strong emotions is not something I enjoy very much."

Involvement scale: Zaichkowsky's (1985) 20-item personal involvement inventory (PII) was considered to measure consumer involvement at the beginning of this research; however, it is not unidimensional both on conceptual and empirical grounds. Mittal (1995) extracted one fundamental factor that contained five items of PII, which were isolated and shown to form a unidimensional scale. According to Mittal (1995), this reduced scale is parsimonious, unidimensional, conceptually sound, and showed the requisite validities. In addition, if judging from the unidimensionality standpoint and simplicity, the new version of PII outperformed the other scales (Mittal, 1995). Therefore, this study used the 5-item scale to measure the consumers' fashion involvement. Consumers were asked to indicate their feelings about apparel by using a 5-point scale. The five items selected from the original 20-items PII scale were: "important to me, of concern to me, means a lot to me, matters to me, and significant to me."

Chapter 2
Review of Literature

This review presents an overview of literature related to the influence of consumer attitudes on apparel purchase behavior. Sections covered are from the broad view of the consumer attitude to the detail of each factor that will influence consumers' purchase intention and behavior; (1) the history of consumer attitude which included the three components of attitude- cognition, affect, and conation, and two perspectives of attitude formation- tripartitie and unidimensionalist; (2) in order to help the reader to clarify the difference among the common used terms of emotion, affect, and mood, the following section in this review of literature is "differentiating affect, emotion and mood"; (3) after clarifying the term of emotion, some background information on the theories of emotion are introduced; and (4) in this section theories of consumer purchase intention will be introduced. There are two major models in this section which became the main structure of this research; (5) since in the theories of consumer purchase intention the social factor is always treated as a major effect, social factors regarding the family and reference groups are introduced in this section; and (6) this research was conduct in two countries- United States and Taiwan which represent two different cultures, collectivist and individualist; therefore, the culture difference between collectivist and individualist countries will be covered. (7) The other topic of this research is individual differences in the need of cognition, emotional, and fashion involvement which has been found to influence consumer behavior will be covered in this section; and (8) the last section is the apparel shopping attributes of atmospheric effect and apparel attributes. These attributes were used to examine consumers' attitude toward apparel shopping.

Consumer Attitude

Historically, two major orientations have emerged in the study of consumer attitudes. The first is often referred to as the *tripartite* view of attitude, because it specifies three underlying components of attitude: cognition, affect, and conation. The cognitive component comprises the knowledge and perceptions that are acquired by a combination of direct experiences with the attitude object and related information from various sources. The affective component encompasses individual's feelings about the attitude object while the conative component is concerned with the likelihood that an individual will behave in a particular way with regard to the attitude object (Schiffman & Kanuk, 2004).

According to Lutz (1990), the second orientation, the unidimensionalist conception of attitude can perhaps best be regarded as an evolution of the tripartite view. The same three components of tripartite attitude appear but the conceptual status is altered significantly. Under the unidimensionalist approach, the cognitive and conative components are "pulled out" of attitude; cognition is relabeled *beliefs* and conation is relabeled *intentions* and *behavior*. Thus, the unidimensionalist position is that attitude is unidimensional, consisting of only one component, affect, which represents the degree of favorability or unfavorability with respect to the attitude object. Other belief and behavioral dimensions are not seen as being components of attitude per se, but rather are viewed as antecedents or consequences of attitude (Fishbein & Ajzen, 1975). While the tripartite view incorporated the notion of consistency among the components, the unidimensionalist view posits a causal flow through the components to account for this consistency. The following section will introduce some theories in both tripartite and unidimensionalist perspective.

Tripartite Perspective-Balance Theory

Several balance models have been developed, all of which are based upon the pioneering work of Heider (1946). According to his balance theory, a person perceives his environment in terms of triads. That is a person views himself as being involved in a triangular relationship in which three elements (persons, ideas, and things) have either positive or negative relationships with each other. This relationship is termed sentiment.

The model is described as unbalanced if any of the multiplicative relationship among the three elements is negative, and balanced if the multiplicative relationship is positive. For example, consider the consumer situation expressed by the following three statements: (1) "I don't like beautiful, luxurious coats", (2) "I like impractical products", and (3) "I think large, luxurious coats are not useful". The triad in following figure describes this situation.

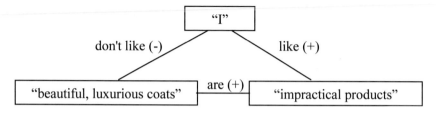

Figure 1 Balance Theory

This structure is not in balance, because there is a positive relationship on two sides of the triad and a negative relationship on the third side. This results in a negative multiplicative product. Because the relationship is unbalanced, it will produce tension for the consumer. It may be possible for her to "live with" the tension and do nothing to resolve it. However, if sufficient tension exits, it is likely that attitude change will occur regarding at least one element in the triad in order to restore balance to the system (Loudon & Della Bitta, 1993).

Tripartite Perspective-Cognitive Dissonance

Festinger developed the theory of cognitive dissonance in 1957. He described cognitive dissonance as a psychological state that results when a person perceives that two cognitions (thoughts), both of which he believes to be true, do not "fit" together; that is, they seem inconsistent. The resulting dissonance produces tension, which serves to motivate the individual to bring harmony to inconsistent elements and thereby reduce psychological tension.

A purchase decision involving choice among brands of chewing gum at a supermarket checkout counter is unlikely to produce much perceptible dissonance. Goods requiring the consumer to commit much of himself or his money, however, are likely to generate considerable post-purchase dissonance. In general, durable and luxury goods are more likely to produce dissonance than are convenience goods, because they usually require larger consumer investment in time, ego, and money (Schiffman & Kanuk, 2004).

Affective-Cognition Consistency Theory

Rosenberg (1956) was particularly concerned with the underlying values of the individual and with how these values related to overall attitude. Therefore, Rosenberg's theory is often identified not only as a consistency theory in tripartite perspective but also as an expectancy-value theory in the unidimentionalist perspective of attitude which will be introduced later. Attitude is the sum of two components in Rosenberg's theory. Value is measured with respect to its value importance (V) to the individual, and its perceived instrumentality (P), that is, the extent to which the value would be blocked or attained by the attitude object in question. The formula is expressed as

$$\text{Attitude} = f \sum_{i=1}^{n} V_i \ P_i$$

where Vi is the measured value importance of the ith value (for example, the value importance of being good looking); Pi is the perceived instrumentality of the attitude object with respect to the ith value (for example, the degree to which using Ultra-white toothpaste blocks or attains being good looking). According to Rosenberg, a change in either attitude or cognitive structure (Pi or Vi) would lead to inconsistency between the two constructs, an inconsistency that would be psychologically uncomfortable for the individual. Therefore, the individual would seek to reduce this inconsistency by bringing attitude more into line with the new cognitive structure, or vice versa. This theory provides an attractive explanation for the origins of attitude. The basic values used to predict attitudes toward any number of objects are the major strength and weakness; the general values while useful in some degree may not be strong predictive then more situation-specific determinants (Lutz, 1990).

Unidimensionalist Perspective- Expectancy-Value Model

The first work on an expectancy-value approach to understanding attitudes was carried out by a group of social psychologists at the University of Michigan (Carlson, 1956; Peak, 1955; and Rosenberg, 1956). The central idea of this model is that one's attitude is a function of one's beliefs, when these beliefs are represented as the sum of the expected values of the attributes ascribed to the attitude object. To predict an attitude, the expectancy and value terms associated with each attribute are multiplied together, and these products are added (Attitude = Σ Expectancy X Value). Instead of using the term "affect," Peak (1955) used the term "evaluation." She defined attitudes as concepts with affective properties and proposed that an attitude is determined by the individual's attitude structure.

Fishbein's Expectancy-Value Model. The development of the expectancy-value approach as a general framework for understanding attitudes was continued by Fishbein (1963), who proposed that attitudes were a function of (a) beliefs about the attitude object, defined as the subjective probability that the attitude object has each attribute, and (b) the evaluative aspect of these beliefs, defined as the evaluation of each attribute. Whereas in Peak (1955), Rosenberg (1956), and Carlson's (1956) formulation, these attributes were goals (or values), Fishbein's more general expectancy-value formulation is expressed algebraically in the following formula:

$$A_O = \sum_{i=1}^{n} b_i \ e_i$$

where Ao is the attitude toward the object, action, or event which can be obtained by calculating the sum of (bi) multiplied by (ei); bi is the belief about the object, action or event; ei is the evaluation of consequence; and n is the number of salient attributes.

Differentiating Affect, Emotion and Mood

Throughout the relevant theory and research literature, the terms "affect," "emotion," and "mood" are frequently used interchangeably (Batson, Shaw, & Oleson, 1992; Cohen & Areni, 1991; Derbaix & Pham, 1998). If distinctions are made at all, they are made on the basis of structural differences, for example, when Schwarz and Clore (1988) distinguish mood from emotion in terms of specificity of target (e.g., moods are diffuse and unfocused; emotions are specific reactions to particular events) and timing (e.g., moods have a cause that is more remote in time than do emotion). While conceptualizations may differ greatly regarding the causes and implications of each of these states, there are some consistent elements among the various definitions. The characteristics tone (positive or negative) and intensity (weak to strong) are noted across affect, emotion, and mood (Batson et al., 1992; Schwarz & Clore, 1988).

Affect

Affect is understood to be the most general term, implying a global state (Batson et al., 1992). In addition, emotion and mood are conceptualized as substates of affect (Batson et al., 1992). Two characteristics, tone, sometimes is referred to as valence or polarity (Plutchik, 1989), may be positive or negative; and intensity refers to the subjective experience of the individual. In their structural conceptualization of affect, Baston et al. (1992) theorized that affect may be seated in the midbrain, informing the individual as to "... those states of affairs that it values more than others. Change from a less valued to a more valued state is accompanied by positive affect. Intensity of the affect reveals the magnitude of the value preference" (p.298). Whether value determines affect, or affect determines value, it is clear, that, without the preferences reflected by positive and negative affect, our experiences would be a neutral gray (Baston et al., 1992; Lazarus & Smith, 1988).

Emotion

Consistent with their functional definitions of affect, emotion and mood, Batson et al., (1992) indicated that introducing a goal moved the level of basic affect to the level of emotion; emotion is most directly related to goal-driven behavior, especially the possibility of obtaining a goal of interest and a perceived change in the individual's relationship to that goal. Furthermore, Schwarz and Clore (1988) made a distinction between moods and emotions. According to their analysis, moods are general positive or negative feelings that people have at a particular time (e.g., being in a good or bad mood). In contrast, emotions such as anger and jealousy are more distinctive in tone and have an identifiable cause.

Several theorists have tried to group emotions and generated the basic emotions for all human's sentiment. Izard (1977) identified ten fundamental emotions: anger, contempt, disgust, distress, fear, guilt, interest, joy, shame, and surprise, each of which he proposed is present to a greater or lesser degree in each emotional experience. More recently, Panksepp (1982) suggested four basic emotions (expectancy, fear, rage, and panic) as did Kemper (1987) (fear, anger, depression, and satisfaction), and Plutchik (1989) indicated eight primary emotions. The divergence of opinion about the number of basic emotions is matched by the divergence of opinion about their identity. Some lists of basic emotions include terms that are included in no other list (Ortony & Turner, 1990).

Mood

Mood is considered to be the lowest level of affective state. As with general affect and emotion, mood states are also characterized by tone and intensity. Mood has been noted to be a milder state that may influence, but not disrupt, cognitive and behavioral processes (Ger, 1989). Several conceptualizations of mood note that this state is more diffuse, and the individual may not always understand its causes. Some theorists note that even relatively small, minor events can heighten or re-orient mood: "It does not require life-shaking affect-laden events… to influence how one behaves, thinks, decides and creates" (Fiske & Taylor, 1991, p. 440). "These apparently insignificant events are capable of influencing our thoughts, motivations and behavior…" (Isen, 1989, p. 91). Events as small as free cookies distributed in a library's study hall, success or failure at a computer game and musical selections in a store (Isen et al., 1976; Alpert & Alpert, 1990) can produce positive or negative moods.

Contrary to the belief that individuals may be unaware of a mood state, functional theory suggests mood has a strong orienting feature in that the individual senses the possibility of pleasure or pain from physical or social cues in the environment (Batson et al., 1992). They also theorize that negative moods are self-correcting, along with a tendency to prefer positive rather than negative moods. Moreover, Gardner (1985) conceptualized mood as having potential impact on the strategic marketing variables of service encounters, point of purchase stimuli and marketing communication.

Theories of Emotion

Background information on the theories of emotion are introduced in this review of literature as emotional response is one of the factors tested in the study. Lazarus (1991) states that theory of emotion must address three parts: relational, motivational and cognitive. Relational emotions are about person-environment relationships that involve harm or benefits and each emotion has its own particular person-environment relationship. Motivational acute emotions are reactions to our desired goals during encounters with the environment. Cognitive emotions are experienced following cognitive appraisals of an encounter. In addition to these facts, Lazarus (1991) demonstrates there is a recursive relationship between cognition and emotion. Cognition can cause emotions following an appraisal, but emotions can in turn affect future cognitions.

Cognition-Emotion Relationship Theories

Attributional Theory. Weiner's attributional theory is a broad category of theories concerned with describing how individuals explain their own and others' behaviors and the consequences of these explanations (Booth Davies, 1992). According to attribution theory, the consequences of a causal attribution are determined by the location of the attribution along three-dimensional continua. The three causal dimensions are locus of causality, controllability, and stability (Weiner, 1985). Locus is the degree to which the behavior or event is judged to be a reflection of characteristics of the target versus characteristics of the target's situation. The controllability causal dimension is the degree to which the behavior or event is judged to be under the volition of the target. The third causal dimension, stability, is the degree to which the behavior or event is judged to be immutable versus changing over time. For instance, anger has been associated with dimensional attributions of external locus and controllability, and guilt has been associated with internal locus and controllability. According to Weiner's theory (Weiner, 1985) the attributional judgments about these three causal dimensions collectively generate emotions and attitudes toward the target. In addition, these feelings and attitudes in turn direct the behaviors of the perceiver (Weiner, 1995).

Appraisal Model. Appraisal is an evaluation of what one's relationship to the environment implies for personal well-being. The model proposed by Smith and Lazarus (1990) described appraisal at two complementary levels of analysis. At a molecular level, appraisal components represent the specific questions evaluated in appraisal. At a molar level, core relational themes synthesize the pattern of evaluation outcomes across the appraisal components into the central meanings underlying the various emotions. The components of primary appraisal are motivational relevance and motivational congruence. The components of secondary appraisal are accountability, problem-focused coping potential, emotion-focused coping potential, and future expectancy.

Emotion Scales

Marketers that most often borrow from psychology are following three typologies of emotion: (1) Mehrabian and Russell's (1974) Pleasure, Arousal, and Dominance (PAD) dimensions of response which represent the premier measure in the field of environmental psychology for assessing individuals' emotional responses to their environment; (2) Izard's (1977) ten fundamental emotions from his Differential Emotions Theory which includes a number of negative emotions (such as anger, disgust and guilt) that are not captured in the PAD and Plutchik scales; and (3) Plutchik's (1980) eight basic emotion categories as the root of all human emotional responses. Havlena and Holbrook (1986) compared the Plutchik and the Mehrabian and Russell (M-R) schemes with respect to consumption experiences. Their results supported use of the Mehrabian-Russell PAD dimensions. However, Machleit and Eroglu (2000), who examined these three emotions scales in a shopping context, found that Izard and Plutchik emotion scales could capture more information about the emotional character of the consumer experience than M-R schemes. In addition to these three emotion scales, Richins (1997) developed a Consumption Emotion Set (CES) to assess the range of emotions most frequently seen in consumption situations based on M-R schemes (1974), Plutchik's (1980) eight basic emotion categories and Izard's (1977) ten fundamental emotions.

Theories of Consumer Purchase Intention

Several theories have been developed to predict consumer behavior intention. In this section, we will compare the Theory of Reasoned Action, the Theory of Planned Behavior, and the Triandis Model as frameworks considered for this study on consumer research in apparel.

Theory of Reasoned Action

According to Fishbein and Ajzen (1975), the Theory of Reasoned Action (TRA) explains an individual's intention toward the enactment of a behavior as a function of the individual's beliefs about engaging in the behavior, as well as that of other important people (subjective norm). Attitudes represent overall evaluations of the behavior as positive or negative for the individual. Thus, individuals are more likely to intend to perform a behavior if they have a positive attitude towards it. Subjective norm (SN) represents the influence of "important others" and is the function of two subcomponents: (1) associated normative beliefs (NB) which is the respondent's belief that the referent approves or does not approve of the behavior; and (2) the consumer's motivation to comply (MC) with salient referents. In figure 2, the subcomponents NB and MC will lead to subjective norm; the beliefs (B) that the behavior leads to certain outcomes and evaluation (E) of the outcomes will lead the attitude toward the behavior. The two components (attitude toward the behavior & subjective norm) will then deliberate the consumer behavior intentions that have direct relationship to consumer behavior.

Ajzen and Fishbein (1980) state that with this theory they can "account for behavior of various kinds by reference to a relatively small number of concepts" (p. 4). They also claim that although "there may ... be certain individuals for whom the theory does not apply ... the accumulating evidence suggests ...that the theory is useful for most individuals and with respect to most social behaviors" (p. 245). A number of empirical studies have incorporated TRA to examine consumer intentions toward shopping. For instance, Shim and Drake (1990), Moore (1990), Evans, Christiansen, and Gill (1996), and Vijayasarathy and Jones (2000) have adapted TRA in their study of electronic shopping, generic prescription drug purchasing, mall shopping, and Internet shopping respectively. In addition, Sheppard, Hartwick and Warshaw (1988) investigated the effectiveness of the TRA model by conducting meta-analyses and found that it has strong predictive utility, even when it is used to investigate situations and activities that do not fall within the boundary conditions originally specified for the model.

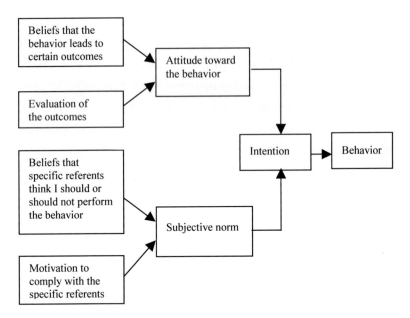

Figure 2   Theory of Reasoned Action (This figure is adapted from
Ajzen and Fishbein, 1980, Figure 7.1, p.84)

After the meta-analysis research of past studies utilizing the Theory of Reasoned Action model, Sheppard, et al. (1988) suggested appropriate modification of the original TRA model to include goal intentions, choice situations, and differences between intention and estimation measures. The model, though tested cross-culturally (Davidson & Thompson, 1980), has also been criticized for assuming Western perspectives on time orientation, probabilistic thinking, and locus of control (Cote & Tansuhaj, 1989). The normative components of the model have also been challenged as representing a Western view of normative influence (Lee & Green, 1990).

Theory of Planned Behavior. The theory of planned behavior (Ajzen & Madden, 1986) extends the theory of reasoned action by introducing an additional construct, the perceived behavior control. The perceived behavioral control is the person's belief as to how easy or difficult performance of the behavior is likely to be. Perceived behavioral control is a function of control beliefs (CB) and perceived facilitation (PF). The following figure demonstrated the relationship among attitude, subjective norm, and perceived behavior control constructs to behavior intention and behavior concepts. Control belief is the perception of the presence or absence of requisite resources and opportunities needed to carry out the behavior. Perceived facilitation is one's assessment of the importance of those resources to the achievement of outcomes (Ajzen & Madden, 1986). The Theory of Planned Behavior (TPB) has been successfully applied to various situations in predicting the performance of behavior and intentions, such as predicting user intentions to use new software (Mathieson, 1991), to perform breast self-examination (Young et al., 1991), and to avoid caffeine (Madden et al., 1992).

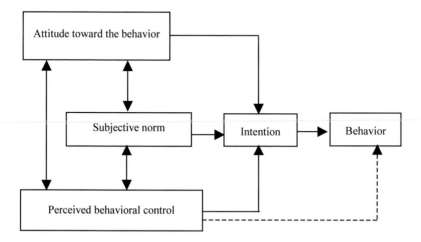

Figure 3   Theory of Planned Behavior (The figure is adapted from Ajzen, 1991, Figure 1, p.182)

Triandis Model

The Triandis model has two equations. The first equation, $P_a = (w_H H + w_I I)$ F, predicts behavior as determined by habit (H), intention (I) and facilitating (F) conditions. The second equation, $I = W_s$ (S) $+ W_a$ (A) $+ W_c$ (C), indicates "I" is the intention function of social (S), affective (A), and consequences (C) factors (Triandis, 1977). Paralleling the Theory of Reasoned Action (Ajzen & Fishbein 1980), the Triandis model treats attitude toward the act and social-normative considerations as determinants of intentions. However, departing from the TRA model, Triandis separated attitude toward the act into two terms: affect toward the act and the value of the perceived consequences of the act. The perceived consequences (C) term thus corresponds to Fishbein and Ajzen's behavioral beliefs, but the Theory of Reasoned Action does not include Triandis's affective term, which he defined as "the particular configuration of emotions [that] becomes activated at the thought of the behavior" (Triandis, 1977, p.16).

Moreover, in the Triandis model, the affect and cognition directly influence intention and are not mediated by an attitude component. For the normative influence Triandis held that social factor (S) incorporates several underlying constructs, including role perceptions, norms, the situational self-concept, and personality. The operational definition of this construct, however, was not well specified (Sheth, 1982; Triandis, 1977, 1982). According to Triandis (1982), the S-component can be measured by asking the person how he/she should act, the A-component by asking for semantic differential judgments on pure affect scales (e.g., enjoyable) related to the act, and the C-component by the usual probability and value judgments in subjective utility research. In operationalizing the model's constructs, Triandis suggests that the constructs are theoretical and can be operationalized in several ways. Triandis (1982, p.152) suggested, "It is highly desirable that multi-method measurement be applied to each construct." Triandis (1982) recommends a global measure for Social factors that focuses on what one should or should not do in a particular context. This incorporating of contextual information into the measures made the model more culturally sensitive and more applicable across cultures (Malhotra & McCort, 2001). Past research with this model revealed that, though it often predicted intention and behavior well, it did not predict intention and behavior consistently better than the TRA (Eagly & Chaiken, 1993).

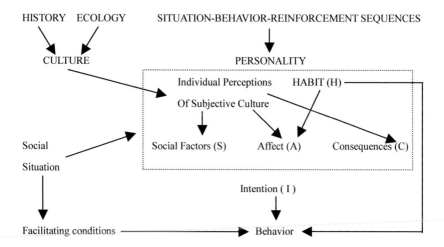

Figure 4 Triandis' Framework

Consumer Behavior in Social Factors

The processes by which people develop their values, motivations, and habitual activity are called socialization (Blackwell, Miniard & Engel, 2001). The family is the first and typically the most powerful socialization influence, then other social norms such as peers, classmates, roommates, college and spouse. Both Fishbein and Ajzen (1980) and Triandis (1982) included the social factor in their consumer purchase intention models. Triandis held that the social factor (S) incorporated several underlying constructs, including role perceptions, norms, the situational self-concept, and personality. Fishbein and Ajzen (1980) used subjective norms to represents the influence of "important others" in social factor. In this research we examined the consumer social group influence in norms, such as family, peers, and girl/boyfriend. Furthermore, we included consumers' demographic, culture, need for cognition, need for emotion, and fashion involvement as their individual differences influence.

Family and Reference Groups Influences

According to Sillars (1995), parents and other family members serve as channels of information, sources of social pressure, and support for one another; it creates a distinct lifestyle, pattern of decision-making, and style of interacting. Children have continuous opportunities to learn and internalize the beliefs, attitudes, and values they have observed, accepting these as the norms (Sears, 1983). Woodson, Childers, and Winn (1976) study of auto insurance found that 62% of men in their twenties reported they have used the same insurance company that their fathers did. Moreover, Arndt (1972) studied agreement between college students and their parents on dimensions of innovativeness, opinion leadership, and loyalty proneness and found strong correlation. Carlson, Laczniak, Grossbart (1994) found that products more visible to children at home have more preference similarity associated with the child's choice rules and beliefs. Heckler, Childers, and Arunachalam (1989) found purchase similarities and observed stronger impacts in parent-child intergenerational influences for convenience goods than for shopping goods. Childers and Rao (1992) assessed reference group effects and pointed out that a family's impact will differ from that of peers depending on whether a product is publicly or privately consumed.

A reference group is an actual or imaginary individual or group conceived of having significant relevance upon an individual's evaluations, aspirations, or behavior (Park & Lessig, 1977). According to Park & Lessig (1977) reference groups influence our fashion and clothing choice in three ways: (1) informational influence which is when the individual seeks information about various brands from an association of professionals or independent group of experts; (2) utilitarian influence which is the individual's decision to purchase a particular brand influenced by their preferences; (3) value-expressive influence which is when the individual feels that the purchase or use of a particular brand will enhance the image others have of him or her. Others (Gergen & Gergen, 1981; Harold, 1965; Smucker & Creekmore, 1972) classified reference group influences as normative and comparative. Normative influence is where the reference group helps set and enforce fundamental standards of conduct as it gives reinforcement and criticism to the individual. Comparative influence means decisions about specific brands are affected as individuals compare themselves to group members.

Reference group influences are not equally powerful for all types of products and consumption activities. Bearden and Etzel (1982) found people are influenced more by reference groups under two situations: (1)

luxuries rather than necessities product purchases, and (2) socially conspicuous or merchandise visible to others. Social referent influence refers to the extent to which relevant others are instrumental in determining an individual's consumption behavior. The behavioral intentions approach used in the current research traditionally has termed this concept, the subjective norm. Subjective norms are the consumer's overall perceptions of what relevant individuals think he or she should do (Ryan, 1982).

Yet, when apparel and other accessories were investigated, most studies purchase intention in the U.S. obtained opposite findings (Casselman & Damhorst, 1991; Chang, Burns, & Noel, 1996; DeLong, Minshall, & Larntz, 1987). For U.S. college students, the purchase intention for unisex shirts was explained more by attitude toward purchasing than subjective norms (Casselman & Damhorst, 1991). Similar findings were obtained for brand name casual apparel (Chang et al., 1996), sweaters (DeLong et al., 1987), and sneakers (Lee & Green, 1991). However, when it comes to studies using the Fishbein model with Asian cultures, Chan and Lau (1998) found that Chinese consumers' intentions to purchase traditional gold rings were influenced more by subjective norms than by attitude. Lee and Green (1991) obtained a similar finding with Korean intentions to purchase sneakers. Shen, Dickson, Lennon, Montalto, and Zhang (2003) added the acculturation variable in the Fishbein Intention model and found the acculturation characteristics did improve the explanation of Chinese apparel purchase intentions for U.S.-made apparel.

The Influence of Culture on Consumer Behavior

Perhaps the most important dimension of cultural difference is that of individualism and collectivism (Hofstede, 2001; Triandis, 1995). It can be explained that people in a collectivistic culture are more concerned with others' reaction and the significance of personal relationships than are people in individualistic cultures (Yang, 1992). Members of individualist cultures (e.g., the United States, Australia, and Canada) tend to hold an independent view of the self that emphasize separateness, internal attributes, and the uniqueness of individuals. In contrast, members of collectivist cultures (e.g., Hong Kong, China, Taiwan, and Japan) tend to hold an interdependent view of the self that emphasizes connectedness, social context, and relationships (Triandis, 1995). This difference suggests that Chinese might be more inclined than Americans to use others' behaviors as a basis for deciding whether to purchase clothing for the following two reasons. First, Chinese might be more likely than Americans to consider others' decisions to be more valid than their own. Second, Asians may consider it more desirable to behave similarly to others as an end in itself independent of this clothing purchase behavior.

Asians tend to be particularly concerned about negative consequences of their behavior (Briley & Wyer, 2001), and often behave in ways that minimize the likelihood of these consequences (Briley & Wyer, 2002). In contrast, Westerners are more inclined to base their behavioral decisions on the benefits they might receive without considering the costs that might occur. Although the cultural differences described above seem plausible, the generality of their effects is unclear. For one thing, cultural differences in normative beliefs and values may only influence people's decisions when situational factors call these norms to their attention (Fong & Wyer, 2003). In Briley & Wyer (2001) study, cultural differences in choice behavior were evident only under conditions in which culture-related decision criteria were likely to be salient. Moreover, situational factors that invoke alternative criteria for decisions can sometimes override the influence of culture-related norms and values (Briley & Wyer, 2002).

Individual Differences

According to Sheth, Mittal and Newman (1999), individual traits consist of unique biogenic and psychogenic aspects of an individual customer. The biogenic individual trait is called "genetics", such as gender, race, and age that all humans inherit from birth. On the other hand, the psychogenic individual traits, called "personality traits," on the other hand are produced by a combination of genetics, group traits, and a person's external environment. In the following section we will cover the fashion involvement, the need for cognition and the need for emotion as individual differences in this study.

Apparel Involvement

According to Zaichkowsky (1985), involvement is defined as "a person's perceived relevance of the object based on their inherent needs, values, and interests" (p. 342). The word object is used in the generic sense and refers to a product, an advertisement, or a purchase situation. Three antecedents of involvement are person factors, object or stimulus factors and situational factors. The evidence of these factors influencing the consumer's level of involvement or response to products, advertising, and purchase decisions is found in the literature. Wright (1974) found variation in the type of media influenced the response given to the same message (object factors). Clarke and Belk (1978) demonstrated that different purchase situations for the same products caused differences in search and evaluation or raised the level of involvement (situational). Lastovicka and Gardner (1978) demonstrated that the same product has different involvement levels across people.

In addition, difference has been found between males and females in their involvement levels (Browne & Kaldenberg, 1997), and age also has been identified as an important dimension in fashion clothing (Fairhurst, Good, & Gentry, 1989). Involvement is the heart of the person-object relationship and the relational variable is most predictive of purchase behavior (Martin, 1998; Evrard & Aurier, 1996). Krugman (1965) described involvement as having two experiences, low involvement and high involvement. Low involvement was characterized by a lack of personal involvement, while high involvement was characterized by a high degree of personal involvement. Involvement has been discussed and utilized to examine fashion clothing in a number of prior studies (Browne & Kaldenberg, 1997; Fairhurst et al., 1989; Flynn & Goldsmith, 1993; Tigert, Ring, & King, 1976). The highly fashion involved consumer has historically been important to fashion researchers and marketers, because they are seen as the drivers, influentials and legitimists of the fashion adoption process (Goldsmith, Moore, & Beaudoin, 1999; Tigert et al., 1976). The nature and role of fashion clothing and its function for individuals have also been shown to result in major differences between the fashion involvements across cultures (Tigert, King, & Ring, 1980), that US consumers have lower fashion involvement than do Dutch consumers. Clothing theorists have devoted considerable attention to understanding the motivations and fashion innovators' behavior focusing on a wide range of topics such as values, attitudes and behaviors.

However, little work has been done on fashion involvement relative to consumer effective response in attitude behavior model in cross culture.

Need for Cognition

The need for cognition refers to an individual's tendency to engage in and enjoy effortful cognitive endeavors (Cacioppo & Petty, 1982). Research on the need for cognition suggests that this characteristic is predictive of the manner in which people deal with tasks and social information (Cacioppo & Petty, 1982). In addition, the need for cognition scale has been frequently used in consumer research in examining the effects of persuasive arguments (Haugtvedt, Petty, Cacioppo, & Steidley, 1988) and advertisement price promotion (Inman, McAlister, & Hoyer, 1990).

Apparel Shopping Attributes

There are many attributes might influence consumer's attitude toward apparel shopping, after review many research, in the following section we will cover two categories for apparel shopping attributes: atmospheric effects and apparel merchandise attributes.

Atmospheric Effects

After reviewing sixty published empirical studies on the influence of marketing atmospherics on consumers, Turley and Milliman (2000) categorized atmospheric variables into five categories. The first category of external variables included the storefront, marquee, entrances, display windows, building architecture, the surrounding area, and parking. Ward, Bitner, and Barnes (1992) examined the prototypicality of a store design; Edwards and Shackley (1992) investigated the effects of exterior window displays. Both researchers found that external variables have an influence on the behavior of retail consumers. The second category was general interior variables, which included design factors such as flooring, lighting, cleanliness, color usage, and ambient factors (e.g., scents, sounds, and temperature). Akhter, Andrews, and Durvasula (1994), Donovan and Rossiter (1982), and Donovan, Rossiter, Marcoolyn, and Newdale (1994) all found that general perceptions of the interior influence approach/avoidance, time spent in the environment and sales.

The third category, store layout and design variables was related to consumers' store knowledge, including fixtures, allocation of floor space, department location, traffic flow, placement of equipment, cash registers, and placement of merchandise. Smith and Burns (1996) studied the optimal use of a power aisle in a warehouse grocery store that is used to display large quantities of a small number of products to create the impression that the products are offered at extremely low prices. Moreover, Iyer (1989) reported that unplanned purchases were higher when consumers have lower knowledge of store layout/design and no time pressure conditions.

The fourth category, point-of-purchase and decoration variables, includes product displays, point-of-purchase displays, price displays, posters, signs, cards and wall decorations. Studies found product displays can significantly influence sales (Gagnon & Osterhaus, 1985; Wilkinson, Mason, & Paksoy, 1982). Patton (1981) reported that the amount of information in the sign can influence sales. Finally, the last category, human variables, included customer crowding, privacy, customer characteristics, personnel/employee characteristics and employee uniforms. Research shows that perceived crowding has a negative influence on consumer evaluations of the shopping experience (Eroglu & Machleit, 1990). In addition, Baker, Levy, and Grewal (1992) found that the more social cues present in the store environment, the higher subjects' arousal. In this research, fourteen apparel shopping attributes such as parking, lighting, ambient factors, design factors, and personnel characteristics were adopted from Shim, Soyeon, and Kotsiopulos (1992), Grewal (1992), Heitmeyer and Kind (2004), Pauline and Geistfeld (2003), Wakefield and Baker (1998), and Durvasula (1994).

Apparel Merchandise Attributes

Many researchers have investigated evaluative criteria related to clothing. Evaluative criteria were defined as "the particular dimensions or attributes that are used in judging the choice alternatives" (Engel, et al., 1995). The most frequently used clothing attributes examined by researchers have been price, style, quality, size/fit, color, fabric, brand name, and country of origin (Cassill & Drake, 1987; Davis, 1987; Eckman, Damhorst, & Kadolph, 1990; Jenkins, 1973; McLean, Roper, & Smothers,, 1986; Workman, 1990).

Lee and Burns (1993) found significant differences in the importance placed on clothing attributes between Korean and United States female undergraduate students. Female college students from the United States indicated fashion and attractiveness were more important than did female college students from Korea. Additionally, in Hsu & Burns's (2002) research, Taiwanese consumers placed more importance on appropriateness for campus wear and where the garment was manufactured, while Americans gave higher scores in size/fit, comfort, and quality in clothing attribute. However, there was no difference in the most important evaluative which was size/fit in clothing attribute between Taiwanese and United States students (Hsiao, 1993; Hsu & Burns, 2002). Additionally, Wang and Heitmeyer (2006) found people in Taiwan had a higher apparel attitude toward US-made apparel than domestic-made apparel regarding the following attributes, "care instruction label, colour, quality, apparel fibre content, fashionableness, attractiveness, brand name, and comfort." This research selected a few apparel attributes to measure consumers' apparel shopping attitude, including quality, price, brand selection, and merchandise variety.

Theoretical Framework

This research will use the Theory of Reasoned Action (TRA) and the Triandis model as the framework which have been found to have strong predictive utility in many research studies. The TRA explains an individual's intention toward the enactment of a behavior as a function of the individual's beliefs about engaging in the behavior, as well as the influence of other important people (subjective norm). Paralleling the TRA model, the Triandis model also treats attitude toward the act and social-normative considerations as determinants of intentions. However, departing from the TRA model, Triandis separated attitude toward the act into two terms: affect toward the act and the value of the perceived consequences of the act.

Summary

To summarize, this review of literature addressed the following topics; (1) the history of consumer attitude which included the tripartite perspective and the unidimensionalist perspective; (2) differentiating affect, emotion and mood, which are frequently used interchangeably; (3) background information on the theories of emotion; (4) theories of consumer purchase intention in TRA, TPB and the Triandis model; (5) consumer behavior in social factors regarding the family and reference groups' influences; (6) the influence of culture on consumer behavior in collectivist and individualist countries; (7) individual differences in the need for cognition, the need for emotion, and fashion involvement; and (8) apparel shopping attributes in atmospheric effect and the apparel attributes. All of these categories will be used to test the hypotheses used in the study.

Chapter 3
Research Methods

This chapter includes a discussion of (1) questionnaire development, (2) pre-test, (3) sample selection, (4) data collection, and (5) data analysis. The research framework is depicted in Figure 5. The three independent variables of the research were: consumers' apparel shopping attitude; consumers' emotional responses while shopping; and subjective norms of social factors. The three moderating variables of the research were: individual differences in the need for cognition, the need for emotion, and apparel involvement. The two dependent variables of the research were: consumer apparel purchase intention and apparel purchase behavior. The purpose of this study was to examine the relationship between these dependent and independent variables for U.S. and Taiwanese consumers.

Questionnaire Development

Since data were collected in Taiwan and U.S. for a cross-cultural comparison, an English version of the questionnaire was developed first and then translated into Chinese. A bilingual English-speaking Chinese graduate student back-translated the questionnaire into English to insure the questionnaire's validity. To increase the validity in the actual consumption of apparel purchase behavior, data were gathered before and after the consumer's next apparel shopping trip.

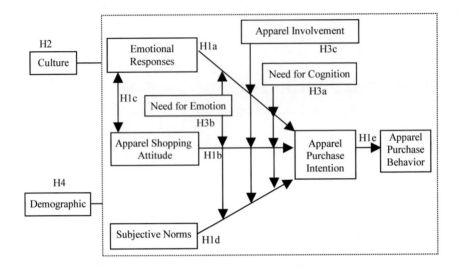

Figure 5 Study Framework

A website questionnaire was design to collect both U.S. and Taiwan data for this research [http://group.kh.usc.edu.tw/teacher/yun/]. The website address and instructions of how to answer the self-report questionnaire online were given to respondents in classes at large U.S. and Taiwan universities. There were three parts of the questionnaire in this online survey. When respondents first entered the website, they needed to choose either "English" or "Chinese 中文" to start the survey. The cover letter was presented after they selected their language. To start the questionnaire, respondents were asked to state their email addresses as the ID for later entry. Part I of the questionnaire covered consumers' individual differences in the need for cognition, the need for emotion, apparel involvement, and consumers' beliefs about the importance of 18 apparel shopping attributes. Respondents started to fill out the first part of the questionnaire after they logged in to the web page and entered their e-mail address. Part II of the questionnaire covered consumers' expectation of their apparel purchase intention for their next apparel shopping trip. In the instructions, respondents were asked to answer this portion right before they went apparel shopping. By doing this, respondents needed to re-enter their ID which was the e-mail address they entered the first time. The last part of the questionnaire needed to be completed after the consumers' apparel shopping trip. The last part included the actual apparel purchase behavior, the consumers' evaluation of their apparel purchase based on the same 18 apparel-shopping attributes, the subjective norms, and demographic factors. The website questionnaire and cover letter for both English and Chinese versions are included in Appendix 2.

In part I of the questionnaire, individual differences in the need for cognition, need for emotion, and apparel involvement were measured. The original need for cognition (NFC) scale was developed by Cacioppo and Petty (1982) which is comprised of 34 items. An 18-item short form for assessing the need for cognition with high internal consistency reliability of .90 was develped by Cacioppo, Petty, and Chuan in 1984. This research adopted Caciopoop, Petty, and Chuan's (1984) short form of the original NFC scale that contains 18 items on a 5-point Likert scale. The respondents would indicate their agreement to the need for cognition from 1 (*strongly disagree*) to 5 (*strongly agree*). The need for emotion (NFE) is defined as "the tendency or propensity for individuals to seek out emotional situations, enjoy emotional stimuli, and exhibit a preference to use emotion in interacting with the world" (Raman, Chattopadhyay, & Hoyer, 1995, p. 537). The NFE scale is composed of 12 items scored on a five-point Likert scale ranging from 1 (*strongly disagree*) to 5 (*strongly agree*). For instance, one item asks respondents to indicate their agreement to "experiencing strong emotions is not something I enjoy very much."

"Fashion involvement" represents another factor that may influence the information processing of subjects (Bagozzi, 1992; Shim et al., 1989). Since Zaichkowsky's (1985) 20-item personal involvement inventory (PII) was used frequently and was used in many cross-cultural studies, it was considered for measuring consumer involvement. However, according to Mittal (1995) the PII is not unidimensional both on conceptual and empirical grounds. Mittal (1995) extracted one fundamental factor that contains five items of PII which were isolated and shown to form a unidimensional scale. This reduced scale is parsimonious, unidimensional, conceptually sound, and showed the requisite validities. In addition, if judging from the unidimensionality standpoint and simplicity, the new version of PII outperformed the other scales (Mittal, 1995). Therefore, in this study we used the five-item PII scale to measure the consumers' involvement of apparel. This scale is composed of a 5-semantic differential item scored on a 5-point scale. For instance, consumers would be asked to rate their apparel involvement from 1 (*unimportant to me*) to 5 (*important to me*). Other items selected from the original 20-item PII scale are: of concern to me, means a lot to me, matters to me, and is significant to me. In addition, consumers' beliefs of the importance on the 18 apparel shopping attributes were measured in part I of the questionnaire. The importance placed on these 18 apparel shopping attributes was used to examine consumers' attitude toward apparel shopping with consumers' evaluation of the same 18 apparel shopping attributes. The evaluation of these attributes was included in part III of the questionnaire.

In part II of the questionnaire, consumers' apparel purchase intention was measured by using four items of a 5-point semantic differential scale. Before their shopping trip, consumers were asked to indicate their apparel purchase intention by using the following items: "unlikely/likely, impossible/possible, improbable/probable, and uncertain/certain to buy." This scale has been used by Oliver and Bearden (1985), Shimp and Sharma (1987), and Yi (1990), and has shown consistently high reliability. In addition to this scale, two items that independently measure consumer intention were included: (1) consumers' beliefs regarding their purchase intention for apparel today and (2) consumers' opinions of the goal for today's shopping trip, whether browsing, buying a specific item, or both.

Consumers were asked to complete part III of the questionnaire after a shopping trip. Respondents would indicate their apparel purchase behavior by stating either she/he did or did not make a purchase today. Instead of a single question regarding the consumers' apparel purchase behavior, multiple questions were used to increases reliability. An additional question about how many pieces of apparel she/he purchased today was asked. In the third part of the questionnaire, respondents were asked to evaluate the 18 apparel shopping attributes. Their beliefs (B) in the importance placed on 18 apparel-shopping attributes (measured in Part I) and evaluation (E) of these attributes being present when they shopped for apparel they purchased or not purchase (measured in Part III) were used to calculate consumers' attitude toward apparel shopping in this study. These 18 apparel shopping attributes were selected on the basis of the review of literature in the store environment and service which were found to be most important and most frequently used by researchers (Baker, Grewal, & Parasuraman, 1994; Oliver, 1994; Pauline & Geistfeld, 2003; Shim & Kotsiopulos, 1992; Wakefield & Baker, 1998).

After evaluating the apparel shopping attributes, respondents were asked to think about how they felt regarding the shopping trip they made. The 17 emotional adjectives which were adopted from the Richins (1997)'s Consumption Emotion Set (CES) were used to measure the consumers' emotional responses while shopping for apparel. One item was deleted from the CES scale, named "other items: guilty, proud, eager, relieved" because of confusing and conflicting wording. Respondents indicated their feeling on a five-point scale from 1 (*not at all*) to 5 (*very strongly*) to express how strongly they felt about each of the emotion adjectives. For instance, consumers would circle number 5 (*very strongly*) if they felt joyful and pleased when they shopped for apparel.

Also in part III, respondents would rank their salient reference, which is the most important person they seek advice from, while they are shopping for apparel. They were asked to indicate the three most important people, for instance, girl/boyfriend "1," followed by parents "2," and then sales associate "3." After they identified their salient references, the subjective norm influence was measured by using the TRA operational concept which is a function of (1) normative beliefs which is the person's belief that the salient referent thinks he/she should (or should not) perform the behavior, and (2) his/her motivations to comply to that referent's opinion (Ajzen & Fishbein, 1980). Normative beliefs of important others (NB) were measured with three items: (a) Do your family members support your apparel purchasing? (b) Do your friends (including boy/girlfriend) support your apparel purchasing behavior? (c) Do salespersons support your apparel purchasing behavior? The respondent would indicate their normative beliefs through a five-point scale from 1 (*not at all*) to 5 (*strongly support*). Motivation to comply (MC) was measured by asking the participants: (a) How often do your family members' opinions influence your apparel purchase decisions? (b) How often do your friends' opinions influence your apparel purchase decisions? (c) How often do your salespersons' opinions influence your apparel purchase decisions? Respondents will indicate their motivation to comply by a-five point scale from 1 (*not at all*) to 5 (*very often*). Three items were used to measure motivation to comply and normative beliefs, rather than the one item recommended by Ajzen and Fishbein (1980) because of concerns with diminished reliability when using one-item measures (Babbie, 2001). The summation of outcomes of normative beliefs multiplied by motivation to comply represents the subjective norm (SN) (Ajzen & Fishbein, 1980). The last section of the questionnaire covered respondents' demographic factors of age, gender, household income, education, and occupation.

Pre-test

Human subject clearance was gained for this study in April, 22, 2004 (Appendix 1). The English version of the questionnaire was given to participants in a six-state graduate consortium which was held at Florida State University to ensure the questionnaire's face validity; the Chinese version of the questionnaire was given to students in a department seminar at the University of Taiwan to ensure the Chinese questionnaire's face validity. Some revisions of wording were made after the pre-test.

Sample Selection

Convenience samples from students of large U.S. and Taiwan universities were used in this research. Online website questionnaires [http://group.kh.usc.edu.tw/teacher/yun/] were designed in both Chinese and English versions in order to do the comparison of two cultures. Even though convenience samples were used for this research, students in different majors from different levels of courses were selected in both Taiwan and U.S. universities.

Data Collection

Since Christmas shopping and returning from the holiday season in the U.S. and Chinese New Year shopping (February, 9th) in Taiwan may cause consumers to change their apparel shopping behavior, data collection for both U.S. and Taiwan was started after March 2005 in the spring semester. Students completed the questionnaires during one semester period. During a semester period the questionnaires were completed by students in different classes at large U.S. and Taiwan universities. Although this was a convenience sample, these consumers were appropriate for the topic, and the data were thought to be suitable for use in a theory testing study such as this one (Calder, Philips, & Tybout 1981). According to Calder and colleagues (1981) homogenous samples are desired for two reasons. First, sample homogeneity helps to reduce error variance that can be attributed to non-theoretical constructs and therefore reduces the likelihood of making a Type II error. When respondents are homogenous with respect to the characteristics that affect their responses, the error variance is reduced and the sensitivity of statistical tests in identifying significant relationships increases. Homogenous respondents are also desired because they permit more exact theoretical predictions than what might be possible with a heterogeneous group. Increased variability in behavior associated with a heterogeneous group makes precise predictions more difficult and thus makes the failure of the theory more difficult to detect.

In an attempt to enhance data quality, two items were included in the questionnaire so as to guard against random responding (Dollinger & DiLalla 1996, pp. 169-171). The first item: "I have tried to answer all of these questions honestly and accurately" with a five-point response format where 1 = *Strongly Disagree* and 5 = *Strongly Agree* was included in a list of scale items for the present study. The second item is: "If you read this item, do not respond to it," with a five-point response format where 1= *Very Unlikely* and 5 = *Very Likely*. Originally 496 completed surveys were received from U.S. and 450 completed surveys were received from Taiwan. The questionnaires in which respondents answered with a "1" or "2" to the first item or recorded a response to the second item were removed from the data set as "unusable" respondents. This left 410 usable questionnaires for U.S. and 353 for Taiwan.

Data Analysis

At the beginning, factor analysis was used to assess the discriminate validity of all the variables in this dissertation. Alpha reliability analysis for each variable scale was also conducted to secure the quality of the research. Descriptive data analysis, bivariate correlations analysis, regression analysis, independent samples *T*-test analysis and multivariate analysis of variances were used to examine the research hypotheses.

Regression analysis was used to examine the following hypotheses for objective one; Hypothesis 1a, which stated that the emotional responses while shopping for apparel will have an effect on the apparel purchase intention of consumers; Hypothesis 1b, which stated that the attitudes of consumers toward apparel shopping will have a positive effect on consumer' apparel purchase intention; and Hypothesis 1d, which stated that the subjective norm will have a positive effect on the apparel purchase intention of consumers. Regression analysis can explain the amount of variance shared in consumers' attitudes toward shopping apparel, subjective norms, and emotional responses for consumers' apparel purchase intention. Additional mediating regression analysis to examine the effect of purchase intention on purchase behavior was conducted for Hypothesis 1e, which stated that consumer purchase intention will have a mediating effect on the apparel purchase behavior and the variables of purchase antecedent, such as consumers' attitude toward shopping apparel, emotional responses, and subjective norms. In Hypotheses 1a, 1b, and 1d, consumers' attitude toward apparel shopping, consumer emotional responses while shopping, and the subjective norms were the independent variables and consumers' apparel purchase intention was the dependent variable. In Hypotheses 1e, the role of consumers' apparel purchase intention changed from dependent variable to mediating variable, and consumer apparel purchase behavior was the dependent variable.

The independent samples T-test analysis was used to examine the hypotheses in objective two, whether U.S. and Taiwan consumers exhibit any cultural difference in their apparel purchase antecedents and apparel purchase behavior; Hypothesis 2a: The subjective norm will have more influence on purchase intention of Taiwan consumers which are collectivist than on purchase intention of U.S. consumers which are individualist; Hypothesis 2b: Consumer attitudes toward apparel shopping will have more influence on purchase intention of Taiwan consumers which are collectivist than on purchase intention of U.S. consumers which are individualist; and Hypothesis 2c: Consumer emotional responses while shopping will have more influence on purchase intention of Taiwan consumers which are collectivist than on purchase intention of U.S. consumers which are individualist. This statistical method can detect the differences between U.S. and Taiwan consumers' apparel purchase behavior antecedents and outcomes of consumers' purchase intention.

Hierarchical moderated regression analysis is used to examine moderating variables; therefore, it was used to examine the following hypotheses for individual differences in objective three; Hypothesis 3a, which stated that the need for cognition of consumers will have a moderating effect on their apparel purchase intention and apparel purchase antecedents such as attitude toward shopping apparel, emotional responses, and social factors; Hypothesis 3b, which stated that the need for emotion of consumers will have a moderating effect on their apparel purchase intention and apparel purchase antecedents such as attitude toward shopping apparel, emotional responses, and social factors; and Hypothesis 3c, which stated that the level of consumers' apparel involvement will have a moderating effect on their apparel purchase intention and apparel purchase antecedents such as attitude toward shopping apparel, emotional responses, and social factors. If the moderating effect of the individual differences did exist, the figure would be plotted to explore the form of the interaction.

Hypothesis four, which stated that the demographic variables of consumers in U.S. and Taiwan will be related to their attitude toward apparel shopping, emotional responses, subjective norms, apparel purchase intention, and apparel behavior, was examined by using multiple variance analysis (*MONOVAs*) to see if these variables made any contribution to the shared variance in the dependent variables.

Chapter 4
Data Analysis and Results

The purpose of this study was to examine the emotional responses while consumers are shopping; consumer attitudes toward apparel shopping; subjective norm; individual differences; and demographic factors for Taiwan and U.S. consumers' apparel purchase intentions and purchase behavior. The purpose was further divided into four objectives. The first objective was to investigate the relationships among apparel purchase behavior, apparel purchase intention and the variables of apparel purchase antecedents such as consumers' attitude toward shopping apparel, emotional responses, and social factors for U.S. and Taiwanese consumers. The second objective was to examine whether U.S. and Taiwan consumers exhibit any cultural difference in their apparel purchase antecedents and apparel purchase behavior. The third objective was to examine the moderating effect of individual differences in the need for cognition, the need for emotion and apparel involvement on their apparel purchase intention. The fourth objective was to examine the demographic factors of age, gender, occupation, income, and education level. The hypotheses for this study were as follows:

Hypothesis 1a: The emotional responses while shopping for apparel will have an effect on the apparel purchase intention of consumers.

Hypothesis 1b: The attitudes of consumers toward apparel shopping will have a positive effect on consumer' apparel purchase intention.

Hypothesis 1c: Apparel shopping attitude factors of store ambience and services will have significant correlations to consumers' emotional responses.

Hypothesis 1d: The subjective norm will have a positive effect on the apparel purchase intention of consumers.

Hypothesis 1e: Consumer purchase intention will have a mediating effect on their apparel purchase behavior and the variables of purchase antecedent such as consumers' attitude toward shopping apparel, emotional responses, and subjective norms.

Hypothesis 2a: The subjective norm will have more influence on purchase intention of Taiwan consumers which are collectivist than on purchase intention of U.S. consumers which are individualist.

Hypothesis 2b: Consumer attitudes toward apparel shopping will have more influence on purchase intention of Taiwan consumers which are collectivist than on purchase intention of U.S. consumers which are individualist.

Hypothesis 2c: Consumer emotional responses while shopping will have more influence on purchase intention of U.S. consumers which are individualist than on purchase intention of Taiwan consumers which are collectivist.

Hypothesis 3a: The need for cognition of consumers will have a moderating effect on their apparel purchase intention and apparel purchase antecedents such as attitude toward shopping apparel, emotional responses, and social factors.

Hypothesis 3b: The need for emotion of consumers will have a moderating effect on their apparel purchase intention and apparel purchase antecedents such as attitude toward shopping apparel, emotional responses, and social factors.

Hypothesis 3c: The level of consumers' apparel involvement will have a moderating effect on their apparel purchase intention and apparel purchase antecedents such as attitude toward shopping apparel, emotional responses, and social factors.

Hypothesis 4: The demographic variables of consumers in U.S. and Taiwan will be related to their attitude toward apparel shopping, emotional responses, subjective norms, apparel purchase intention, and apparel behavior.

This chapter will first cover information about sample characteristics, measurement scale characteristics, descriptive statistics, reliabilities, and correlations for the research variables. Then the analysis methods for examining the research hypotheses follow which are: linear regression for hypotheses 1a, 1b, and 1d; bivariate correlation analysis for hypothesis 1c; mediation regression for hypotheses 1e; and hierarchical moderated regression for hypotheses 3a, 3b, and 3c for both Taiwan and U.S. data. The results for the research hypotheses are discussed at the end of the data analysis for each country. Hypotheses 2a, 2b, and 2c were examined after hypotheses 1a, 1b, 1c, 1d, 1e, 3a, 3b, and 3c, because hypotheses 2a, 2b, and 2c were comparisons between U.S. and Taiwan consumers. The Statistical Package for the Social Sciences 11.5 (SPSS) for Windows was used to analyze numerical data.

Sample Characteristics

Table 1.1 presents the descriptive analysis for the U.S. sample characteristics. The U.S. sample consisted of 362 (88.3%) females and 48

(11.7%) males with most ages ranging from 18 to 24 (n = 385, 93.9%). There were 306 (74.6%) whites, 44 (10.7%) African-Americans, 44 (10.7%) Hispanics, and 16 (4%) Asians. Two hundred and seventeen (52.9%) respondents indicated they had either part-time or full time jobs and 193 (47.1%) respondents were unemployed. The average household income in the sample was in the range of $70,000 to $84,999 US dollars and the highest frequency in the income level was "more than $115,000 US dollars" (n = 110, 26.8%).

Table 1.1   Description of U.S. Respondents (N = 410)

U.S.	Response %	Response Total
Gender: Male	11.7%	48
Female	88.3%	362
Total	100%	410
Race: White/Caucasian	74.6%	306
African American/Black	10.7%	44
Hispanic/Latino	10.7%	44
Asian American/Asian	4%	16
Total	100%	410
Employment: Unemployed	47.1%	193
Employed	52.9%	217
Total	100%	410
AGE: 18-24	93.9%	385
25-31	5.9%	24
32-38	0.2%	1
Total	100%	410
Income level: < $9,999	11.7%	48
$10,000 - $24,999	8.3%	34
$25,000 - $39,999	7.1%	29
$40,000 -$54,999	8.0%	33
$55,000 - $69,999	9.5%	39
$70,000 - $84,999	7.8%	32
$85,000 - $99,999	6.8%	28
$100,000- $114,999	13.9%	57
$ More than 115,000	26.8%	110
Total	100%	410
Student level: Undergraduate	94.6%	388
Graduate	5.4%	22
Total	100%	410

Table 1.2 presents the descriptive analysis for the Taiwan sample characteristics. The Taiwan sample consisted of 247 (70%) females and 106 (30%) males with most ages ranging from 18 to 24 ($n = 321$, 90.9%). Two hundreds and sixty (73.7%) respondents indicated they were unemployed and 93 (26.3%) were employed. The average household income in the sample was in the range of $23,000 to $28,999 US dollars and the highest frequency in the household income level was "less than $17,000 US dollars" ($n = 123$, 34.8%).

Table 1.2   Description of Taiwan Respondents ($N = 353$)

Taiwan	Response %	Response Total
Gender: Male	30%	106
Female	70%	247
Total	100%	353
Resident area: North	27.5%	97
Middle	17.8%	63
South	54.7%	193
Total	100%	353
Employment: Unemployed	73.7%	260
Employed	26.3%	93
Total	100%	353
AGE: 18-24	90.9%	321
25-31	5.9%	21
32-38	3.3%	11
Total	100%	353
Income level: < $16,999	34.8%	123
$17,000 - $22,999	19.5%	69
$23,000 - $28,999	17.6%	62
$29,000 -$35,999	17.0%	60
$36,000 - $41,999	3.1%	11
$42,000 - $47,999	3.4%	12
$48,000 - $54,999	3%	1
$55,000- $61,999	0	0
$ More than 62,000	4.2%	15
Total	100%	353
Student level: Undergraduate	95.5%	337
Graduate	4.5%	16
Total	100%	353

Measurement Characteristics

With the exception of consumers' apparel shopping attributes, all of the construct measures used in this dissertation are self-reports with multi-item scales chosen because they have been used in other studies and have demonstrated acceptable reliability and validity. Consumers' shopping attitude was measured by multiplying (1) the beliefs of the apparel shopping attributes, and (2) the individual's subjective evaluation of those apparel shopping attributes. Consumers were asked to indicate how important each of the apparel shopping attributes. The belief of the apparel shopping attributes was measured by using a five-point Likert scale from 1 (*very unimportant*) to 5 (*very important*). The evaluation of apparel shopping attributes was measured by asking consumers to indicate their view of perceived consequences of each apparel shopping attribute. The evaluations of each outcome were measured by using a five-point scale from 1 (*very unlikely*) to 5 (*very likely*).

The subjective norm was measured by multiplying (1) Normative beliefs (NB), which is the person's belief that the salient referent thinks he/she should (or should not) perform the behavior, and (2) his/her motivations to comply that referent. Respondents would indicate their normative beliefs with regard to each referent by responding to questions such as: "Do your family members support your apparel purchase behavior?" Respondents' answers were measured on a 5-point scale ranging from 1 (*not at all*) to 5 (*strongly support*). Motivation to comply (MC) was measured by using the same referents in the NB, by answering questions such as: "How often do your family members' opinions influence your apparel purchase decision?" on a 5-point scale, from 1 (*not at all*) to 5 (*very often*).

Consumers' emotional responses while shopping were measured by using Richins's (1997) Consumption Emotion Set (CES), which contains 17 items with a five-point scale from 1 (*not at all*) to 5 (*very strongly*) to express how strongly they felt about each of the emotional responses, e.g., anger, joy, and love. One item was deleted from the CES scale, named "other items: guilty, proud, eager, relieved" because of confusing and conflicting wording, leaving a total of 16 items for consumers' emotional responses.

Consumers' apparel purchase intention was measured by using four items of a 5-point semantic differential scale. Before their shopping trip, consumers were asked to indicate their apparel purchase intention by using the following items: "unlikely/likely, impossible/possible, improbable/probable, and uncertain/certain to buy." This scale has been used by Oliver and Bearden (1985), Shimp and Sharma (1987), and Yi (1990), and has shown consistently high reliability. In addition to this scale, two items that independently measure consumer intention were included: (1) consumers' beliefs regarding their purchase intention for apparel today and (2) consumers' opinions of the goal for today's shopping trip, whether browsing, buying a specific item, or both.

The need for cognition was measured by using an 18-item scale with a five-point Likert response format (coefficient alpha of .90) developed by Cacioppo, Petty, and Chuan (1984). Respondents would indicate their agreement to the need for cognition phrase from 1 (*strongly disagree*) to 5 (*strongly agree*). For instance, one item asks respondents to indicate how they think about themselves, "I would prefer complex rather than simple problems." Higher scores meant consumers have a higher need for cognition. Individual difference in the need for emotion (NFE) was measured by Raman, Chattopadhyay, and Hoyer (1995) scale, which was composed of 12 items with a five-point Likert-type scale ranging from 1 (*strongly disagree*) to 5 (*strongly agree*). For instance, respondents would indicate their disagreement /agreement with "experiencing strong emotions is not something I enjoy very much."

The 5-item scale (Mittal, 1995), which was modified from Zaichkowsky's (1985) original 20-item personal involvement inventory (PII), was used to measure the consumers' fashion involvement. Consumers were asked to indicate their feelings about apparel by using a 5-point scale. The five items selected from the original 20-items PII scale are: "important to me, of concern to me, means a lot to me, matters to me, and significant to me."

Since the apparel shopping attributes for measuring consumers' apparel shopping attitude were selected from different sources and created for this dissertation, exploratory factor analysis (EFA) with oblimin rotation was conducted to determine an appropriate number of factors and the pattern of factor loadings primarily from the data. According to Hair, Anderson, Tatham, and Black (1998) item loading over .50 is very important significance, over .40 is important significance and over .30 is the minimum level of practical significance. In addition, Biomedical Data Processor (BMDP) Statistical Software (1993) stated that based on the different sample size, the requirement of the significant factor loading would be different. If sample size is 200 the factor loading has to be .40 for identifying significance; however, if the sample size is larger than 350, factor loading over .30 is significant.

Table 2.1   Factor Loadings of Apparel Shopping Attributes for Taiwan Data

Variable	Factor 1	Factor 2	Factor 3	Factor 4
Apparel Shopping Attributes	Interior/Exterior Design and Ambience	Convenience for Shopping	Product Quality	Employee Service Quality
A 13 - Interior Decoration	.781			
A14 - Exterior Architecture	.739			
A11- Appropriate Sound	.726			
A10 - Music Selection	.661			
A12 - Lighting	.642			
A1 - Ample Parking		.712		
A2 - Walking Distance		.697		
A4 – Crowding		.586		
A3 - Travel Time to Store		.572		
A5- Space between merchandise		.564		
A7- Variety of Apparel			.773	
A9 - Brand Selection			.655	
A6 - Good Quality			.547	
A8 - Price			.488	
A17 - Sales willing to help				-.781
A16 - Sales' product knowledge				-.697
A15 - No pressure from Sales				-.509
A18 - Appropriate number of sales				-.462
% of variance explained	21.7%	13.3%	7.1%	5.6%

Note. N = 353. Extraction Method: Principal Axis Factoring. Rotation Method: Oblimin with Kaiser Normalization. Loadings under .30 are suppressed. The total percent of variance explained by these four factors is 47.7%. For detail items please see Appendix 2- questionnaire.

Both countries samples sizes in our dissertation (U.S. $N = 410$; Taiwan $N = 353$) were larger than 350 which means the factor loading over .30 identifies significance on a .05 alpha level with a power level of 80 percent. There were four factors extracted for the apparel shopping attributes in both U.S. (61.6% of variance explained) and Taiwan (59% of variance explained) data. These four factors were (1) product quality (good quality, variety, price, and brand); (2) employee service quality (sales personnel friendly, product knowledge, willingness to assist, and amount of employees); (3) ambience and interior/exterior design of the store (music, lighting, interior decoration and exterior architecture); and (4) convenience of shopping (parking, distance, travel time, crowding, walking space in store, and waiting time). For the Taiwan data, all the item loadings were significant and over the required .30 loading. However in the U.S. data, one problematic item was deleted due to double loading of two factors (A15 - sales personnel are not giving me pressure to buy). Table 2.1 presents the exploratory factor analysis for the apparel shopping attributes for Taiwan data and Table 2.2 presents the exploratory factor analysis for the U.S. data.

Table 2.2 Factor Loadings of Apparel Shopping Attributes for U.S. Data

Variable	Factor 1	Factor 2	Factor 3	Factor 4
Apparel Shopping Attributes	Product Quality	Convenience for Shopping	Interior/Exterior Design and Ambience	Employee Service Quality
A7- Variety of Apparel	.933			
A6 - Good Quality	.829			
A9 - Brand Selection	.668			
A8 - Price	.592			
A2 - Walking Distance		.796		
A1 - Ample Parking		.707		
A3 - Travel Time to Store		.526		
A4 - Crowding		.441		
A5- Space between merchandise		.339		
A 13 - Interior Decoration			.693	
A14 - Exterior Architecture			.683	
A10 - Music Selection			.683	
A11- Appropriate Sound			.655	
A12 - Lighting			.554	
A17 - Sales willing to help				-.853
A16 - Sales' product knowledge				-.800
A18 - Appropriate number of sales				-.792
A15 - No pressure from Sales	.359			-.433
% of variance explained	42.8%	7.3%	6.9%	3.5%

Note. N = 410. Extraction Method: Principal Axis Factoring. Rotation Method: Oblimin with Kaiser Normalization. Loadings under .30 are suppressed. The total percent of variance explained for these four factors is 60.5%. For detail items please see Appendix 2- questionnaire. Item 15 was removed due to cross-loading in two different factors.

Other responses from the measurement scales were submitted to a principal components factor analysis (PC) with varimax rotation in order to assess the discriminant validity, which assures that the items load in the designated variables. All variables in the dissertation accounted for a single factor except for the consumer emotional responses while shopping which counted for two factors – positive and negative emotions. Table 3.1 presents factor loadings of variable items for U.S. data, and Table 3.2 presents factor loadings of variable items for Taiwan data. In the U.S. data all the item loadings were significant (loading > .30). However, in the Taiwan data four items were deleted. Three items (cog 7, cog16, and emo10) were deleted because the loadings were less than .30 and therefore insignificant. The other item was deleted (shoemo9) because it cross-loaded for two factors.

Table 3.1 Factor Loadings of Variable Items for U.S. Data

Item	Factor 1	Factor 2	Factor 3	Factor 4	Factor 5	Factor 6	Factor 7
Att 6	.838						
Att 7	.822						
Att 17	.803						
Att 16	.795						
Att 15	.781						
Att 8	.759						
Att 18	.748						
Att 4	.712						
Att 12	.699						
Att 5	.672						
Att 13	.647						
Att 9	.592						
Att 1	.567						
Att 14	.552						
Att 11	.531						
Att 10	.446						
Att 2	.398						
Att 3	.371						
Cog2		.716					
Cog4		.713					
Cog5		.655					
Cog3		.650					
Cog12		.646					
Cog13		.614					
Cog11		.613					
Cog17		.598					
Cog14		.589					
Cog10		.578					
Cog15		.552					
Cog6		.518					
Cog7		.494					
Cog1		.450					
Cog16		.448					

Cog9		.421					
Cog8		.413					
Cog18		.353					
Emo12			.732				
Emo9			.731				
Emo8			.713				
Emo3			.712				
Emo11			.689				
Emo2			.653				
Emo5			.647				
Emo4			.646				
Emo6			.630				
Emo1			.609				
Emo10			.578				
Emo7			.510				
Shoemo14				.835			
Shoemo12				.805			
Shoemo13				.800			
Shoemo15				.792			
Shoemo11				.735			
Shoemo10				.668			
Shoemo16				.591			
Shoemo9				.578			
Int3					.842		
Int2					.830		
Int6					.750		
Int4					.743		
Int5					.617		
Int1					.416		
Inv3						.848	
Inv4						.826	
Inv5						.751	
Inv2						.655	
Inv1						.598	
Shoemo4							.681
Shoemo5							.645
Shoemo1							.599
Shoemo2							.586
Shoemo3							.583
Shoemo6							.558
Shoemo8							.466
Shoemo7							.434

Note. $N = 410$. Extraction method: Principal component analysis. Rotation method: Varimax with Kaiser Normalization. Loadings greater than .30 are shown. For detail variable items please see Appendix 2-questionnaire.

Table 3.2   Factor Loadings of Variable Items for Taiwan Data

Item	Factor 1	Factor 2	Factor 3	Factor 4	Factor 5	Factor 6	Factor 7
Att 13	.731						
Att 6	.686						
Att 14	.674						
Att 12	.624						
Att 5	.604						
Att 8	.568						
Att 16	.554						
Att 11	.548						
Att 4	.536						
Att 7	.521						
Att 18	.515						
Att 17	.513						
Att 10	.485						
Att 15	.460						
Att 1	.419						
Att 9	.411						
Att 2	.383						
Att 3	.365						
Cog2		.745					
Cog10		.689					
Cog4		.677					
Cog5		.665					
Cog3		.664					
Cog11		.650					
Cog15		.634					
Cog6		.605					
Cog13		.593					
Cog1		.573					
Cog9		.499					
Cog14		.486					
Cog18		.478					
Cog8		.408					
Cog17		.357					
Cog12		.335					
Cog7		<.30					
Cog16		<.30					
Shoemo4			.849				
Shoemo5			.843				
Shoemo6			.835				
Shoemo3			.750				
Shoemo8			.715				
Shoemo1			.691				

Shoemo7			.678				
Shoemo2			.629				
Shoemo14				.887			
Shoemo13				.882			
Shoemo15				.871			
Shoemo12				.831			
Shoemo10				.706			
Shoemo16				.668			
Shoemo9			.429	.557			
Shoemo11				.497			
Int3					.886		
Int4					.857		
Int2					.835		
Int6					.500		
Int5					.489		
Int1					.413		
Inv4						.829	
Inv3						.819	
Inv5						.649	
Inv1						.586	
Inv2						.528	
Emo12							.651
Emo2							.638
Emo3							.629
Emo9							.581
Emo8							.558
Emo11							.517
Emo6							.496
Emo5							.478
Emo1							.452
Emo7							.429
Emo4							.309
Emo10							<.30

Note. $N = 353$. Extraction method: Principal component analysis. Rotation method: Varimax with Kaiser Normalization. Loadings less than .30 will be deleted. Cross loading- item that has significant loadings on more than one factor will be deleted. Cognition items 7, 16 and Emotion item 10 would be deleted due to the factor loadings are not significant. The shopping emotion item 9 would be deleted due to the cross loading on both positive and negative factors. For detail variable items please see Appendix 2-questionnaire.

Descriptive Statistics, Reliabilities, and the Correlations

Bivariate correlations analysis was used as a preliminary test to examine the relationships between the independent variables and the dependent variables. Most scales ranged from 1-5, except "consumers' apparel shopping attitude" and "subjective norm" which ranged from 1-25, and "purchase behavior" which ranged from 1-2. Table 4.1 presents descriptive statistics, reliabilities, and correlations among the research variables for the U.S. sample. Many significant relationships were found among variables related to apparel purchase intention of consumers (e.g. involvement, subjective norms, and positive emotions when consumers are shopping). In addition, the positive emotions when consumers are shopping had significant relationships among subjective norms of consumers ($r = .16$, $p < .01$) and apparel shopping attitude of consumers ($r = .20$, $p < .01$). However, no relationships were found among apparel shopping attitude of consumers, apparel purchase intention of consumers ($r = .04$), and purchase behavior of consumers ($r = .08$).

Most of the expected correlations were found among the research variables. For instance, the negative correlation between negative emotions while shopping and positive emotions while shopping ($r = -.24$, $p < .01$); the positive correlation between consumers' apparel purchase intention and consumer purchase behavior ($r = .39$, $p < .01$); and the positive correlation between consumers' need for cognition and need for emotion ($r = .25$, $p < .01$). Furthermore, consumers' need for emotion correlated positively with their apparel involvement ($r = .20$, $p < .01$) and their apparel shopping attitude ($r = .12$, $p < .05$). Regarding the demographic variables, in the U.S. data, female consumers tended to have higher scores on the need for emotion ($r = .19$, $p < .01$); higher apparel involvement ($r = .26$, $p < .01$); higher subjective norms ($r = .13$, $p < .01$);

higher attitude scores in apparel shopping ($r = .15$, $p < .01$); higher negative emotions when they are shopping ($r = .11$, $p < .01$); and higher intention to purchase apparel ($r = .13$, $p < .01$) than male consumers. However, none of the other demographic variables, employment level, age level, income level, and student level came out significant.

Table 4.1   Descriptive Statistics and Correlations of Variables for U.S. Samples

Variable	Mean	SD	α	1	2	3	4	5	6	7	8	9
1. NFC	3.29	.52	.87									
2. NFE	3.30	.62	.89	.25**								
3. INV	3.11	.86	.82	-.02	.20**							
4. ATT	13.68	3.65	.87	.04	.12*	-.01						
5. SN	12.02	3.64	.72	-.07	.09	.02	.06					
6. PSHOEM	2.77	.87	.88	.03	.04	.03	.20**	.16**				
7. NSHOEM	1.36	.41	.72	-.01	-.03	.07	-.14**	-.02	-.24**			
8. PI	3.48	.71	.85	-.04	.10	.28**	.04	.14**	.20**	-.06		
9. PUR	1.77	.42	None	-.08	-.01	.01	.08	.14**	.23**	-.13**	.39**	
10. Gender	1.88	.32	None	-.10	.20**	.26**	.15**	.13**	.08	.11*	.13**	.03

Note. Listwise excluded, $N = 410$. **$p < .01$. *$p < .05$, two-tailed. NFC (need for cognition), NFE (need for emotion), INV (apparel involvement), ATT (apparel shopping attitude = attributes importance X attributes evaluation), SN (subjective norm = normative beliefs X motivation to comply), PSHOEM (positive emotions when consumers are shopping), NSHOEM (negative emotions when consumers are shopping), PI (purchase intention), and PUR (purchase behavior).

Table 4.2 presents descriptive statistics, reliabilities, and correlations among the research variables for the Taiwan samples. Many significant relationships were found among research variables. The dependent variable, apparel purchase intention of the consumer, was significantly positive correlated with need for cognition ($r = .19$, $p < .01$), apparel involvement ($r = .25$, $p < .01$), attitude toward apparel shopping ($r = .16$, $p < .05$), and positive emotions while shopping ($r = .30$, $p < .01$). Apparel purchase behavior of the consumer was significantly correlated with need for emotion ($r = .11$, $p < .05$), apparel involvement ($r = .15$, $p < .01$), positive emotions while shopping ($r = .23$, $p < .01$), negative emotions while shopping ($r = -.22, p < .01$), and apparel shopping intention ($r = .52$, $p < .01$). In addition, subjective norms of consumers had significant relationships among apparel involvement of consumers ($r = .16, p < .01$) and apparel shopping attitude of consumers ($r = .22, p < .01$). However, no relationship was found between consumers' subjective norms and their apparel purchase intention. Other significant correlations were found between positive emotions while shopping and the need for cognition of consumers ($r = .20, p < .01$); positive emotions while shopping and apparel involvement of consumers ($r = .13, p < .05$); positive emotions and apparel shopping attitude ($r = .19, p < .01$); and positive emotions and consumers' subjective norm ($r = .14, p < .01$). Furthermore, consumers' need for emotion had negative correlation with their apparel shopping attitude ($r = -.12, p < .05$) and positive correlation with the need for cognition of consumer ($r = .14, p < .01$).

Regarding the demographic variable of gender for the Taiwan data, female consumers tended to have higher fashion involvement ($r = .20, p < .01$), higher subjective norms ($r = .20, p < .01$), higher apparel purchase intention ($r = .12, p < .05$), and higher apparel purchase behavior ($r = .13$, $p < .05$) than male consumers. Other expected relationships in the demographic variables included a positive correlation between age and income levels ($r = .23, p < .01$), employment status and income levels ($r = .15, p < .01$), and age and employment status ($r = .35, p < .01$). However, there was no statistically significant difference in gender across the employment levels ($r = -.07, p > .05$), nor was there a significant association between gender and resident area of students ($r = -.08, p > .05$) in Taiwan. These findings show some correlations among the research variables in this study.

Table 4.2 Descriptive Statistics and Correlations of Variables for Taiwan Samples

Variable	Mean	SD	α	1	2	3	4	5	6	7	8	9
1. NFC	3.27	.51	.85									
2. NFE	1.54	.47	.74	.14**								
3. INV	3.75	.73	.75	.12*	.01							
4. ATT	14.79	3.17	.83	.09	-.12*	.24**						
5. SN	10.47	3.28	.73	.04	-.07	.16**	.22**					
6. PSHOEM	2.82	.86	.89	.20**	-.01	.13*	.19**	.14**				
7. NSHOEM	1.51	.60	.88	.09	-.01	-.03	.01	.07	.15**			
8. PI	3.03	.64	.80	.19**	.05	.25**	.16*	.03	.30**	-.07		
9. PUR	1.56	.50	None	.10	.11*	.15**	.01	.06	.23**	-.22**	.52**	
10. Gender	1.70	.46	None	-.03	.03	.20**	.05	.20**	.10	-.02	.12*	.13*

Note. Listwise excluded, $N = 353$. **$p < .01$. *$p < .05$, two-tailed. NFC (need for cognition), NFE (need for emotion), INV (apparel involvement), ATT (apparel shopping attitude), SN (subjective norm), PSHOEM (positive emotions when consumers are shopping), NSHOEM (negative emotions when consumers are shopping), PI (purchase intention) and PUR (purchase behavior).

Linear Regression Analysis for the Taiwan Data

In this research at the beginning, general linear regression analysis was conducted to examine hypotheses 1a, 1b, and 1d, bivariate correlation analysis for hypothesis 1c, mediation regression analysis for hypotheses 1e, and hierarchical moderated regression analysis for hypotheses 3a, 3b, and 3c for the Taiwan data, followed by the same group of statistical tests to examine the hypotheses for the U.S. data. Hypotheses for objectives two and four were examined after the linear regression analyses for both countries were completed.

General Linear Regression for Hypotheses 1a, 1b, and 1d of Objective One for Taiwan Consumers

The first objective was to investigate the relationships among apparel purchase behavior, apparel purchase intention and the variables of apparel purchase antecedents such as consumers' attitude toward shopping apparel, emotional responses while shopping, and social factors for U.S. and Taiwanese consumers. The linear regression analysis was conducted to examine the H1a, the emotional responses while shopping for apparel will have an effect on their apparel purchase intention, H1b, the attitudes of consumers toward apparel shopping will have a positive effect on consumer' apparel purchase intention, and H1d, the subjective norm will have a positive effect on the apparel purchase intention of consumers, in the research model (please refer to the study framework in p. 42). The information in Table 5.1 presents the significant results ($F = 11.07, p < .01$) from the linear regression. Looking at these four variables, positive emotions when consumers are shopping, negative emotions when consumers are shopping, consumer attitude toward apparel shopping, and subjective norms, revealed that 10% of the variance was explained (Adjusted R Square) by variations in the independent variables in the Taiwan data. Additionally, the t-value was significant for positive emotions when consumers are shopping ($t = 5.66, p < .01$), and negative emotions when consumers are shopping ($t = -2.20, p < .05$). This evidence gave support for the H1a, the emotional responses while shopping for apparel will have an effect on their apparel purchase intention. In addition, the t-value was significant for consumer attitude toward apparel shopping ($t = 2.20, p < .05$) which supported H1b, the consumer attitude toward apparel shopping will have a positive effect on consumers' apparel purchase intention. No significant relationship was found for subjective norm ($t = -.64, p > .01$); therefore, H1d, the subjective norm will have a positive effect on apparel purchase intention of consumers was not supported in the Taiwan data. Figure 6 was included to further clarify theses findings of the consumers' apparel purchase intention antecedents for Taiwan consumers.

Table 5.1   Regression Analysis for Hypotheses 1a, 1b, and 1d of the
           Research Model- Taiwan

Model and Variables	df	F	Adjusted R^2	ΔR^2	β
Dependent variable: Purchase Intention	348	11.07**	.103	.113	
Positive emotions while shopping					.220**
Negative emotions while shopping					-.120*
Apparel shopping attitude					.023*
Subjective norm					-.006
Constant					2.319

Note. $N = 353$.   *$p < .05$.   ** $p < .01$. Unstandardized regression coefficients from the last step

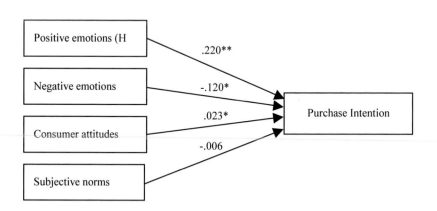

Figure 6   Antecedents of Consumers' Apparel Purchase Intention -
           Taiwan

Bivariate Correlations for Hypothesis 1c of Objective One for Taiwan Consumers

In order to examine the hypothesis 1c, apparel shopping attitude factors of store ambience and service will have significant correlations to consumers' emotional responses (please refer to the study framework in p. 42), additional bivariate correlations analysis for each factor of the apparel shopping attitude was conducted and the results are given in Table 5.2. In previous bivariate correlations analysis (please refer to Table 4.2 on p. 65), attitude toward apparel shopping was used as single variable to examine the correlations with all other research variables, later a factor analysis was conducted and four factors, ambience, convenience, product quality, and service (please refer to Table 2.1 on p. 58), were found underlined the attitude toward apparel shopping variable. Previous research found that service and ambience had positive correlation toward consumers' emotion (Baker et al, 1992; Darden & Babin, 1994); therefore, the additional bivariate correlations analysis needed to be conducted in order to examine the correlations among ambience, service, and emotional responses while consumers are shopping. The apparel shopping attitude factors for the ambience ($r = .14$, $p < .01$) and the service ($r = .14$, $p < .01$) factors were significantly related to positive emotional responses when consumers are shopping. However, both the ambience ($r = .07$, $p > .05$) and the service ($r = .09$, $p > .05$) factors were not significantly related to negative emotional responses when consumers are shopping. Since both the ambience and service factors of consumers' apparel shopping attitude had significant relationships to positive emotional responses while consumers are shopping, and no significant relationship to negative emotional responses while consumers are shopping, Hypothesis 1c was partially supported.

Table 5.2   Descriptive Statistics and Correlations of Apparel Shopping Attitude Factors and Emotional Responses While Taiwan Consumers Are Shopping – Hypothesis 1c

Variable	Mean	SD	1	2	3	4	5	6
1. Product	17.43	4.34						
2. Convenience	14.64	4.55	.37**					
3. Ambience	12.77	4.51	.34**	.30**				
4. Service	16.29	4.52	.38**	.19**	.45**			
5. PSHOEM	2.82	.86	.25**	.06	.14**	.14**		
6. NSHOEM	1.51	.60	-.04	-.05	.07	.09	.15**	
7. Intention	3.03	.64	.17**	.03	.15**	.11*	.30**	-.07

Note. Listwise excluded, N = 353. **p < .01. *p < .05, two-tailed. PSHOEM (positive emotions when consumers are shopping), NSHOEM (negative emotions when consumers are shopping).

Mediation Regression Analysis for Hypothesis 1e of Objective One for Taiwan Consumers

A three-step regression procedure for mediation (Baron & Kenny, 1986) was used to examine hypothesis 1e, consumer purchase intention will have a mediating effect on their apparel purchase behavior and the variables of purchase antecedent such as consumers' attitude toward shopping apparel, emotional responses, and subjective norms. The procedure involves estimating three separate regression equations. First, the independent variables (apparel shopping attitude, positive/negative emotions, and subjective norms) should be significantly related to the mediating variable, which is purchase intention for this research; second, the independent variables (apparel shopping attitude, positive/negative emotions, and subjective norms) should be significantly related to the dependent variable, which is purchase behavior in this research; and third, the mediating variable, consumer purchase intention, should be related to the dependent variable, purchase behavior, with the independent variables, (apparel shopping attitude, positive/negative emotions, and subjective norms) included in the equation. If the first three conditions hold, at least partial mediation is present. If the independent variables have insignificant beta weights in the third step, then complete mediation is present.

The results was shown in Table 6. In the first equation, the mediator was regressed, which is purchase intention in this study, on the independent variables, which are attitude, subjective norm, positive emotions, and negative emotions. Significant results were found for attitude (β= .115, p < .05), positive emotions (β= .296, p < .01), negative emotions (β= -.112, p < .05), but not for subjective norm (β= -.033, p > .05). Next the dependent variable, purchase behavior, was regressed on the independent variables, which are attitude, subjective norm, positive emotions, and negative emotions. The beta weights for positive emotions (β= .275, p < .01) and negative emotions (β= -.259, p < .01) were significant for the second equation. To test the third step of mediation, in equation three we regressed the dependent variable on the mediating variable (purchase intention) with the independent variables (attitude, subjective norm, positive emotion, and negative emotion).

Significant results were found for positive emotion (β= .133, p < .01), negative emotion (β= -.205, p < .01), and purchase intention (β = .482, p < .01). Not all the purchase antecedents had significant effect on all three equations, only the positive emotions and negative emotions were significant in all three equations. Moreover, the beta weights for positive emotions were dropped; therefore, the partial mediation of consumer purchase intention is present for the Taiwan data. In conclusion, partial support was provided for Hypothesis 1e, consumer purchase intention will have a mediating effect on apparel purchase behavior and the variables of purchase antecedent such as consumers' attitude toward shopping apparel, emotional responses, and subjective norms. Figure 7 was included to further clarify theses findings of the mediating effect of consumers' apparel purchase intention on purchase behavior of Taiwan consumers.

Table 6   Regression Analysis for Examining Hypothesis 1e, the Mediating Effect of Purchase Intention on Purchase Behavior- Taiwan

Variable			df	F	Adjusted R^2	β
Equation 1	Dependent Purchase	Independent Intention	348	11.07**	.103	
		Apparel shopping attitude				.115*
		Subjective norm				-.033
		Positive emotions while shopping				.296**
		Negative emotions while shopping				-.112*
2		Purchase Behavior	348	12.12**	.112	
		Apparel shopping attitude				-.049
		Subjective norm				.044
		Positive emotions while shopping				.275**
		Negative emotions while shopping				-.259**
3		Purchase Behavior	347	33.89**		
		Apparel shopping attitude				-.105*
		Subjective norm				.060
		Positive emotions while shopping				.133**
		Negative emotions while shopping				-.205**
		Purchase Intention				.482**

Note. $N = 353$.   *$p < .05$.   ** $p < .01$. Standardized regression coefficients from the last step

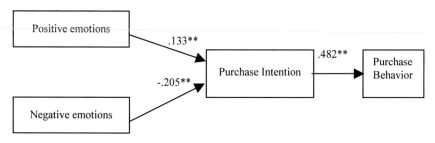

Figure 7   The Mediating Effect of Purchase Intention on Purchase Behavior- Taiwan

Hypotheses 2a, 2b, and 2c for objective two, to examine whether U.S. and Taiwan consumers exhibit any cultural difference in their apparel purchase antecedents and apparel purchase behavior, is discussed after the examination of the individual regression analyses of Hypotheses 3a, 3b, and 3c for the Taiwan and the U.S. data.

Hierarchical Moderated Regression for Hypotheses 3a, 3b, and 3c of Objective Three for Taiwan Consumers

Hierarchical moderated multiple regression analysis (Cohen & Cohen, 1983) was used for objective three, to examine the moderating effect of individual differences in the need for cognition, the need for emotion and apparel involvement on their apparel purchase intention, because this test examine the moderating effect. No significant interactive effects were found from the moderators of the need for cognition and the need for emotion of consumers in the Taiwan data. A significant interactive effect of apparel involvement was found for positive emotions when consumers are shopping and their purchase intention. In the analysis, apparel purchase intention was entered as a dependent variable and centered positive emotions when consumers are shopping as the independent variable in the first step. Centered variables may be used when graphing interactions (Aiken and West, 1991). Centered variables have a mean of 0, but they retain their original standard deviation. Then centered apparel involvement was entered as the moderator in the second step. In the final step the interaction term (centered positive emotion X centered apparel involvement) was entered. The result for the significant interaction effect of apparel involvement on apparel purchase intention is shown in Table 7. The interaction term of positive emotions while shopping and apparel involvement explained a significant incremental portion of variance ($\Delta R^2 = .010$, $p < .05$) for consumers' purchase intention over and above that explained by the main effects of positive emotions while shopping and apparel involvement. Even though both the positive emotion while shopping ($\Delta R^2 = .087$, $p < .01$) and apparel involvement ($\Delta R^2 = .045$, $p < .01$) had main effects on purchase intention, consumers' purchase intention was really dependent upon the interactive effect of positive emotions when consumers are shopping and apparel involvement in Taiwan consumers. Since no significant interactive effects were found from the moderators of the need for cognition and the need for emotion of consumers in Taiwan consumers, hypotheses 3a and 3b were not supported. Hypothesis 3c was supported since a significant interactive effect of apparel involvement was found on positive emotions when consumers are shopping and on their purchase intention. Figure 8 was included to further clarify the moderating effect of consumers' apparel involvement on apparel purchase intention for Taiwan consumers.

Table 7   Hierarchical Moderated Regression Results for Apparel Purchase Intention - Taiwan

Variable	β	t	Adjusted R^2	ΔR^2
Step 1: Independent Variable - Positive Emotions while shopping $F(1, 351) = 33.64$ **	-.153	-.916	.085	.087**
Step 2: Moderator Variable - Apparel Involvement $F(2, 350) = 26.73$**	-.081	-.704	.128	.045**
Model 3: Interaction – Positive emotions while shopping * Involvement $F(3, 349) = 19.26$**	.417*	1.973	.135	.010*

Note: $N = 353$. Unstandardized regression coefficients from the last step. * $p < .05$.   ** $p < .01$. Dependent Variable: Consumers' apparel purchase intention.

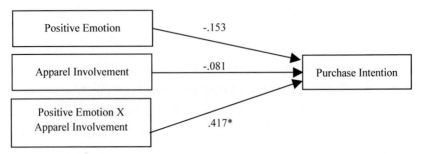

Figure 8 The Moderating Effect of Consumers' Apparel Involvement
on Apparel Purchase Intention - Taiwan

When interaction of the variables occurs, an explanation of these relationships is required. In this study, to explore the form of the interaction, Figure 9 was plotted to show the relationship between high/low levels of positive emotions and high/low level of apparel involvement on consumer purchase intention. This interactive graph illustrates that consumers having low apparel involvement tended to have stronger reactions to positive emotions when they are shopping ($M = 2.55$ when the positive emotions while shopping was high; $M = 3.69$ when the positive emotions while shopping was low) than consumers having high apparel involvement ($M = 3.22$ when the positive emotions while shopping was high; $M = 2.69$ when the positive emotions while shopping was low). Respondents who had low apparel involvement and low positive emotions when they are shopping held the highest level of purchase intention ($M = 3.69$) in Taiwan. On the other hand, the lowest level of consumer purchase intention ($M = 2.55$) was held by those with low apparel involvement and high positive emotions when they are shopping in Taiwan.

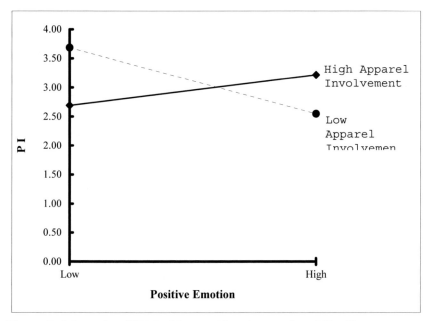

Figure 9 Interactive Effect of Apparel Involvement and Positive
Emotion on Purchase Intention –Taiwan

Since two independent regression analyses were run for Taiwan and
U.S. consumers, the summary of hypothesis tests for objective one and
three is given in Table 8 for Taiwan consumers. Objectives two and four
are examined later in this chapter.

Table 8 Summary of Hypothesis Tests for the Theoretical Model of Antecedents and Outcomes of Consumers' Purchase Intention - Taiwan

Hypotheses	Support for Hypotheses
H1a: The emotions when consumers are shopping for apparel will have an effect on consumers' apparel purchase intention.	Supported
H1b: The consumer attitude toward apparel shopping will have a positive effect on consumers' apparel purchase intention.	Supported
H1c: Apparel shopping attitude factors in store ambience and services will have significant correlations to consumers' emotional responses.	Partial support
H1d: The subjective norm will have a positive effect on consumers' apparel purchase intention.	Not supported
H1e: Consumer purchase intention will have a mediating effect on their apparel purchase behavior and the apparel purchase antecedents such as consumers' attitude toward shopping apparel, emotional responses, and subjective norms.	Partial support
H3a: The need for cognition of consumers will have a moderating effect on their apparel purchase intention and apparel purchase antecedents such as attitudes, emotions, and subjective norm.	Not supported
H3b: The need for emotion of consumers will have a moderating effect on their apparel purchase intention and apparel purchase antecedents such as attitudes, emotions, and subjective norm.	Not supported
H3c: The level of consumers' apparel involvement will have a moderating effect on their apparel purchase intention apparel purchase antecedents such as attitudes, emotions, and subjective norm.	Partial support

Linear Regression Analysis for the U.S. Data

Same as the Taiwan data analysis, this section began with general linear regression analysis to examine hypotheses 1a, 1b, and 1d, bivariate correlation analysis for hypothesis 1c, mediation regression analysis for hypotheses 1e, and hierarchical moderated regression analysis for hypotheses 3a, 3b, and 3c for the U.S. data. Hypotheses for objectives two and four were examined after the linear regression analyses for both countries were completed.

General Linear Regression for Hypotheses 1a, 1b, and 1d of Objective One for U.S. Consumers

The first objective was to investigate the relationships among apparel purchase behavior, apparel purchase intention and the variables of apparel purchase antecedent such as consumers' attitude toward shopping apparel, emotional responses, and social factors for U.S. and Taiwanese consumers. The linear regression analysis was conducted to examine the H1a, the emotional responses while shopping for apparel will have an effect on their apparel purchase intention, H1b, the attitudes of consumers toward apparel shopping will have a positive effect on consumer' apparel purchase intention, and H1d, the subjective norm will have a positive effect on the apparel purchase intention of consumers, in the research model (please refer to the study framework in p. 42). The information in Table 9 presents the significant results ($F = 5.274, p < .01$) from the linear regression. Looking at these four variables, positive emotions when consumers are shopping, negative emotions when consumers are shopping, consumer attitude toward apparel shopping, and subjective norms, revealed that 4% of the variance was explained (Adjusted R Square) by variations in the independent variables in the U.S. data. Additionally, since the t-value was significant only for the positive emotions when consumers are shopping ($t = 3.40, p < .01$), but not for the negative emotions when consumer are shopping ($t = -.391, p > .01$), H1a, the emotional responses while shopping for apparel will have an effect on their apparel purchase intention was partially supported. Since the t-value was significant for the subjective norm ($t = 2.16, p < .05$), H1d, the subjective norm will have a positive effect on apparel purchase intention of consumers, was supported in the U.S. data. No significant results were found for consumer attitude toward apparel shopping ($t = -.068, p > .01$); therefore, H1b, the consumer attitude toward apparel shopping will have a positive effect on consumers' apparel purchase intention, was not supported in the U.S. data. Figure 10 was included to further clarify these findings of the consumers' apparel purchase intention antecedents for U.S. consumers.

Table 9.1   Regression Analysis for Hypotheses 1a, 1b, and 1d of the Research Model- U.S.

Model and Variables	df	F	Adjusted R^2	ΔR^2	β
Dependent variable: Purchase Intention	405	5.274**	.040	.050	
Positive emotions while shopping					.144**
Negative emotions while shopping					-.034
Apparel shopping attitude					-.001
Subjective norm					.021*
Constant					2.881

Note. $N = 410$.   *$p < .05$.   ** $p < .01$. Standardized regression coefficients from the last step

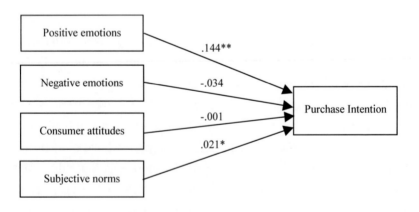

Figure 10 Antecedents of Consumers' Apparel Purchase Intention - U.S.

Bivariate Correlations Analysis for Hypothesis 1c of Objective One for U.S. Consumers

In order to examine hypothesis 1c, apparel shopping attitude factors of store ambience and service will have significant correlations to consumers' emotional responses, additional bivariate correlations analysis for each factor of the apparel shopping attitude was conducted and the results are given in Table 9.2. In previous bivariate correlations analysis (please refer to Table 4.1 on p. 63), attitude toward apparel shopping was used as single variable to examine the correlations with all other research variables, later a factor analysis was conducted and four factors, ambience, convenience, product quality, and service (please refer to Table 2.2 on p. 59), were found underlined the attitude toward apparel shopping variable. Previous research found that service and ambience had positive correlation toward consumers' emotion (Baker et al, 1992; Darden & Babin, 1994); therefore, the additional bivariate correlations analysis needed to be conducted in order to examine the correlations among ambience, service, and emotional responses while consumers are shopping. The apparel shopping attitude factors for the ambience ($r = .23$, $p < .01$) and the service ($r = .11$, $p < .05$) were significantly related to positive emotions when consumers are shopping. Moreover, the apparel shopping attitude factors in the service ($r = -.10$, $p < .05$) was also significantly related to negative emotions when consumers are shopping, but not in the ambience ($r = -.07$, $p > .05$) in the U.S. data. Since both the ambience and service factors of consumers' apparel shopping attitude had significant relationships to positive emotional responses while consumers are shopping, and the service factor also had significant relationships to negative emotional responses, but not in ambience factor, Hypothesis 1c was partially supported for the U.S. data.

Table 9.2 Descriptive Statistics and Correlations of Apparel Shopping Attitude Factors and Emotional Responses While U.S. Consumers Are Shopping - Hypothesis 1c

Variable	Mean	SD	1	2	3	4	5	6
1. Product	17.17	5.13						
2. Convenience	12.13	4.57	.32**					
3. Ambience	11.81	4.56	.38**	.41**				
4. Service	15.44	5.68	.52**	.37**	.46**			
5. PSHOEM	2.77	.87	.17**	.11*	.23**	.11*		
6. NSHOEM	1.36	.41	-.13**	-.11*	-.07	-.10*	-.24**	
7. Intention	3.48	.72	.06	.02	.01	.04	.20**	-.06

Note. Listwise excluded, $N = 353$. **$p < .01$. *$p < .05$, two-tailed. PSHOEM (positive emotions when consumers are shopping), NSHOEM (negative emotions when consumers are shopping).

Mediation Regression for Hypothesis 1e of Objective One for U.S. Consumers

A three-step regression procedure for mediation (Baron & Kenny, 1986) was used to examine hypothesis 1e, consumer purchase intention will have a mediating effect on their apparel purchase behavior and the variables of purchase antecedent such as consumers' attitude toward shopping apparel, emotional responses, and subjective norms. The procedure involves estimating three separate regression equations. First, the independent variables (apparel shopping attitude, positive/negative emotions, and subjective norms) should be significantly related to the mediating variable, which is purchase intention for this research; second, the independent variables (apparel shopping attitude, positive/negative emotions, and subjective norms) should be significantly related to the dependent variable, which is purchase behavior in this research; and third, the mediating variable, consumer purchase intention, should be related to the dependent variable, purchase behavior, with the independent variables, (apparel shopping attitude, positive/negative emotions, and subjective norms) included in the equation. If the first three conditions hold, at least partial mediation is present. If the independent variables have insignificant beta weights in the third step, then complete mediation is present.

The results are shown in Table 10. In the first equation, when the mediator which is purchase intention was regressed on the independent variables which are attitude, subjective norm, positive emotions, and negative emotions, significant results were found for subjective norms (β = .106, $p < .05$) and positive emotions when consumers are shopping (β = .174, $p < .01$), but not for apparel shopping attitude (β = -.003, $p > .05$) and negative emotions when consumers are shopping (β = -.020, $p > .05$). Next the dependent variable, which is purchase behavior, was regressed on the independent variables, which are apparel shopping attitude, subjective norm, positive emotions, and negative emotions. The beta weights for positive emotions (β = .189, $p < .01$) and subjective norm (β = .104, $p < .05$) were significant for the second equation. To test the third step of mediation, in equation three the dependent variable (purchase behavior) was regressed on the mediating variable (purchase intention) with the independent variables (apparel shopping attitude, subjective norm, positive emotions, and negative emotions). Significant results were found in positive emotions (β = .129, $p < .01$) and purchase intention (β = .345, $p < .01$). Since all three equations were significant for the independent variable of positive emotions and the beta weights dropped, partial mediation is present for the U.S. data. In addition, the independent variable of subjective norm has an insignificant beta weight in the third step; therefore, complete mediation is present. Thus partial support was provided for Hypothesis 1e, consumer purchase intention will have a mediating effect on apparel purchase behavior and the variables of purchase antecedent such as consumers' attitude toward shopping apparel, emotional responses, and subjective norms. Figure 11 was included to further clarify these findings of the mediating effect of consumers' apparel purchase intention on their purchase behavior for U.S. consumers.

Table 10   Regression Analysis for Examining Hypothesis 1e, the Mediating Effect of Purchase Intention on Purchase Behavior - U.S.

Variable		df	F	Adjusted R^2	β
Equation 1	Dependent Independent Purchase Intention	405	5.274**	.040	
	Apparel shopping attitude				-.003
	Subjective norm				.106*
	Positive emotions while shopping				.174**
	Negative emotions while shopping				-.020
2	Purchase Behavior	405	7.724**	.062	
	Apparel shopping attitude				.024
	Subjective norm				.104*
	Positive emotions while shopping				.189**
	Negative emotions while shopping				-.081
3	Purchase Behavior	404	18.253**		
	Apparel shopping attitude				.025
	Subjective norm				.068
	Positive emotions while shopping				.129**
	Negative emotions while shopping				- .074
	Purchase Intention				.345**

*Note. N =410. *p < .05. ** p < .01. Standardized regression coefficients from the last step*

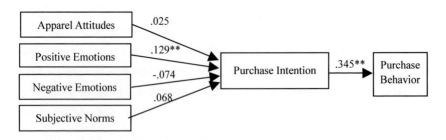

Figure 11 The Mediating Effect of Purchase Intention on Purchase Behavior- U.S.

Hypotheses 2a, 2b, and 2c for objective two, to examine whether U.S. and Taiwan consumers exhibit any cultural difference in their apparel purchase antecedents and apparel purchase behavior, is discussed after the examination of the individual regression analyses of Hypotheses 3a, 3b, and 3c for the Taiwan and the U.S. data.

Hierarchical Moderated Regression for Hypotheses 3a, 3b, and 3c of Objective Three for U.S. Consumers

Hierarchical moderated multiple regression analysis (Cohen & Cohen, 1983) was used for objective three, to examine the moderating effect of individual differences in the need for cognition, the need for emotion and apparel involvement on their apparel purchase intention, because this test examines the moderating effect. No significant interactive effects were found from the moderators of the need for cognition and apparel involvement of consumers in the U.S. data. A significant interactive effect of need for emotion was found for negative emotions while shopping and their purchase intention. In the analysis, apparel purchase intention was entered as the dependent variable and centered negative emotions when consumers are shopping as the independent variable in the first step. Centered variables may be used when graphing interactions (Aiken and West, 1991). Centered variables have a mean of 0, but they retain their original standard deviation. The centered need for emotion was entered as the moderator in the second step. In the final step the interaction term (centered negative emotion X centered need for emotion) was entered. The result for the significant interaction effect is shown in Table 11. The interaction term of negative emotions when consumers are shopping and the need for emotion explained a significant incremental portion of variance ($\beta = .73$, $\Delta R^2 = .027$, $p < .01$) for consumers' purchase intention over and above that explained by the main effects of negative emotions while shopping and the need for emotion. Negative emotions while shopping (β= -.62, p < .01) and need for emotion (β= -.48, p < .01) had main effects on purchase intention only if the interaction effect existed. As the result, consumers' purchase intention was moderated by the negative emotions when consumers are shopping and the need of emotion interactive effect. Additionally, consumers' purchase intention was dependent upon the level of the negative emotions when consumers are shopping and the individual difference in need for emotion. Since no significant interactive effects were found from the moderators of the need for cognition and apparel involvement of consumers in the U.S. data, hypothesis 3a and 3c were not supported. Hypothesis 3b was supported since a significant interactive effect of need for emotion was found on negative emotions while shopping and on their purchase intention. Figure 12 was included to further clarify these findings of the moderating effect of consumers' need for emotion on apparel purchase intention for U.S. consumers.

Table 11   Hierarchical Moderated Regression Results for Apparel Purchase Intention - U.S.

Variable	β	t	Adjusted R^2	ΔR^2
Step 1: Independent Variable - Negative Emotions while shopping $F (1, 408) = 1.68$, ns	-.622**	-3.56	.002	.004
Step 2: Moderator Variable - Need for Emotion $F (2, 407) = 2.69$, ns	.480**	3.79	.008	.009
Step 3: Interaction variable – Negative emotions while shopping X need for emotion $F (3, 406) = 5.65$, **	-.730**	-3.38	.033	.027*

Note: N =410. Unstandardized regression coefficients from the last step. * $p < .05$.   ** $p < .01$. Dependent Variable: Consumers' apparel purchase intention.

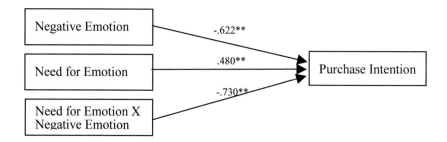

Figure 12 The Moderating effect of the Need for Emotion on Apparel Purchase Intention - U.S.

When interaction of the variables occurs, an explanation of these relationships is required. In this study, to explore the form of the interaction, Figure 13 was plotted to show the relationship between high/low negative emotions and high/low need for emotion on consumer purchase intention. This interactive graph illustrates that consumers with high need for emotion tended to have stronger reactions to negative emotional responses when they are shopping ($M = 2.6$ when the negative emotional responses were high; $M = 5.3$ when the negative emotional responses were low) than consumers with low need for emotion ($M = 3.10$ when the negative emotional responses were high; $M = 2.89$ when the negative emotional responses were low). Respondents who had high need for emotion and low negative emotions when they are shopping held the highest level of purchase intention ($M = 5.3$) in U.S. On the other hand, the lowest level of consumer purchase intention was held by those with high need for emotion and high negative emotions while shopping ($M = 2.6$) in U.S.

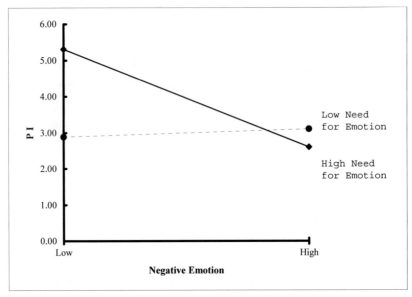

Figure 13 Interactive Effect of Need for Emotion and Negative
Emotions while shopping on Purchase Intention -U.S.

The U.S. data analysis summary of Hypothesis tests for objectives
one and three is presented in Table 12. Compared to the summary Table 8
for Taiwan consumers (please refer to p. 75), the results for hypothesis 1a,
1c, 1e, and 3a are the same. On the other hand, the results for hypothesis
1b, 1d, 3b, and 3c are different.

Table 12　Summary of Hypothesis Tests for the Theoretical Model of Antecedents and Outcomes of Consumers' Purchase Intention - U.S.

Hypotheses	Support for Hypotheses
H1a: The emotions when consumers are shopping for apparel will have an effect on consumers' apparel purchase intention.	Supported
H1b: The consumer attitude toward apparel shopping will have a positive effect on consumers' apparel purchase intention.	Not supported
H1c: Apparel shopping attitudes factors in store ambience and services will have significant correlations to consumers' emotional responses.	Partial support
H1d: The subjective norm will have a positive effect on consumers' apparel purchase intention.	Supported
H1e: Consumer purchase intention will have a mediating effect on their apparel purchase behavior and the variables of purchase antecedent such as consumers' attitude toward shopping apparel, emotional responses, and subjective norms.	Partial support
H3a: The need for cognition of consumers will have a moderating effect on their apparel purchase intention and apparel purchase antecedents such as attitude, emotions, and subjective norm.	Not supported
H3b: The need for emotion of consumers will have a moderating effect on their apparel purchase intention and apparel purchase antecedents such as attitude, emotions, and subjective norm.	Partial support
H3c: The level of consumers' apparel involvement will have a moderating effect on apparel purchase intention and apparel purchase antecedents such as attitude, emotions, and subjective norm.	Not supported

The Independent Samples T-test for Objective Two: the Cultural Difference

The second objective was to examine whether U.S. and Taiwan consumers exhibit any cultural difference in their apparel purchase antecedents and apparel purchase behavior. To examine objective 2, the

Independent Samples T-test was utilized to examine the mean difference between Taiwan and U.S. consumers in all research variables. The results are presented in Table 13, which indicated that only the need for cognition and the positive emotions when consumers are shopping did not have significant mean differences between Taiwan and U.S. consumers. Hypothesis 2a was not supported since U.S. consumers had a higher mean score for the subjective norms than Taiwan consumers, and the mean difference was significant between Taiwan and U.S. consumers ($t = 6.12$, $p < .001$). Moreover, hypothesis 2a can also be analyzed by scanning the results of the regression analysis for Taiwan and U.S data. Since the subjective norms had a positive relationship to consumer apparel purchase intention for the U.S. data, but not for the Taiwan data, Hypothesis 2a which stated that the subjective norm will have more influence on purchase intention of Taiwan consumers which are collectivist than on purchase intention of U.S. consumers which are individualist was not supported.

Table 13　Independent Samples T-test between Taiwanese and U.S. consumers for all research variables

Variable	U.S. Mean (SD)	Taiwan Mean (SD)	Mean differences	t-value
Need for Cognition	3.28 (.52)	3.27 (.51)	0.02	.33
Need for Emotion	3.30 (.62)	1.54 (.47)	1.76	43.58***
Apparel Involvement	3.11 (.86)	3.75 (.73)	-0.64	-10.82***
Apparel Shopping Attitude	13.68 (3.65)	14.79 (3.17)	0.48	-4.42***
Subjective Norm	12.02 (3.64)	10.47 (3.28)	1.55	6.12***
PSHOEM	2.77 (.87)	2.82 (.86)	-0.05	-.88
NSHOEM	1.36 (.41)	1.51 (.60)	-0.15	-4.11***
Purchase Intention	3.48 (.71)	3.03 (.64)	0.45	8.91***

Note. Listwise excluded, $N_{Taiwan} = 353$. $N_{U.S.} = 410$. ***$p < .001$. *SD*, standard deviation, two-tailed. PSHOEM (positive emotions when consumers are shopping). NSHOEM (negative emotions when consumers are shopping).

Hypothesis 2b, consumer attitudes toward apparel shopping will have more influence on purchase intention of Taiwan consumers which are collectivist than on purchase intention of U.S. consumers which are individualist, was supported since we found Taiwan consumers had a higher mean score on apparel shopping attitude ($M_{U.S.}$ = 13.68; M_{Taiwan} = 14.79) and the mean difference was significant between U.S. and Taiwan consumers (t = -4.67, p < .001). Moreover, since consumer attitude toward apparel shopping was found significant for apparel purchase intention by regression analysis for Taiwan consumers but not for U.S. consumers, Hypothesis 2b was supported.

Hypothesis 2c, consumer emotional responses while shopping will have more influence on purchase intention of U.S. consumers which are individualist than on purchase intention of Taiwan consumers which are collectivist, was not supported, since there was no significant mean difference between the positive emotions of U.S. and Taiwan consumers when they were shopping for ($M_{U.S.}$ = 2.77; M_{Taiwan} = 2.82). Additionally, both countries found positive emotions while shopping had a significant positive relationship to apparel purchase behavior by regression analyses. One the other hand, negative emotions while shopping had a significant mean difference between U.S. and Taiwan consumers ($M_{U.S.}$ = 1.36, M_{Taiwan} = 1.51, p < .001). However, Taiwan consumers had a higher score for negative emotions while shopping than U.S. consumers. Therefore, Hypothesis 2c, emotions when consumers are shopping will have more influence on U.S. consumers' purchase intention than Taiwan consumers, was not supported.

Bivariate Correlation Analysis and Multivariate Analysis of Variances for Objective Four

Hypothesis 4, the demographic variables of consumers in U.S. and Taiwan will be related to their attitude toward apparel shopping, emotional responses, subjective norms, apparel purchase intention, and apparel behavior, was partially supported for both U.S. and Taiwan. Significant correlations were found between gender and apparel purchase antecedents and behavior for U.S. and Taiwan consumers (please refer to Table 4.1 on page 63 and Table 4.2 on page 65). In the U.S., female consumers tended to have a higher score for the need for emotion ($r = .19$, $p < .01$), higher subjective norms ($r = .13, p < .01$), a higher attitude score in apparel shopping ($r = .15$, $p < .01$), higher negative emotions when they are shopping ($r = .11, p < .01$), higher apparel involvement ($r = .26$, $p < .01$), and higher apparel purchase intention ($r = .13$, $p < .01$) than male consumers. In Taiwan, female consumers tended to have higher apparel involvement ($r = .20, p < .01$), higher subjective norm ($r = .20, p < .01$), higher apparel purchase intention ($r = .12, p < .05$), and higher apparel purchase behavior ($r = .13, p < .05$) than male consumers.

Additional multivariate analysis of variances (*MANOVAs*) was also used to determine if demographic variables had any relationship to consumer apparel purchase antecedent variables in both U.S. and Taiwan consumers. In U.S. consumers, gender was significantly related to consumers' apparel purchase antecedent variables ($F = 2.60$, $p < .05$, observed power $= .92$). More specifically, gender was significantly related to the individual difference in need for emotion ($F = 5.11$, $p < .05$), apparel involvement ($F = 5.04$, $p < .05$), and the negative emotions when consumers are shopping ($F = 4.20$, $p < .05$). The results are consistent with bivariate correlations analysis which found female consumers tended to have a higher need for emotion ($r = .19$, $p < .01$), higher negative emotions when they were shopping ($r = .11$, $p < .01$), and higher apparel involvement ($r = .26$, $p < .01$).

In Taiwan consumers, gender was also significantly related to consumers' apparel purchase antecedent variables ($F = 3.48$, $p < .01$, observed power $= .98$). More specifically, gender was significantly related to the individual difference in apparel involvement ($F = 10.44$, $p < .01$), subjective norm ($F = 15.17$, $p < .001$), and apparel purchase intention ($F = 3.91$, $p < .05$).The results are consistent with bivariate correlations analysis which found female consumers tended to have higher apparel involvement ($r = .20$, $p < .01$), higher subjective norm ($r = .20$, $p < .01$), and higher apparel purchase intention ($r = .12$, $p < .05$).

Summary of Research Hypotheses

To summarize, four objectives and hypotheses were developed and tested. Of these four, Table 14 (p. 90) contains the summary of hypotheses findings for Taiwan and U.S. data. In the Taiwan data, significant supports were found for H1a, the emotional responses while shopping for apparel will have an effect on their apparel purchase intention; H1b, the attitudes of consumers toward apparel shopping will have a positive effect on consumer' apparel purchase intention; and H2b, consumer attitudes toward apparel shopping will have more influence on purchase intention of Taiwan consumers which are collectivist than on purchase intention of U.S. consumers which are individualist. Partially significant supports were found for H1c, apparel shopping attitude factors of store ambience and services will have significant correlations to consumers' emotional responses; H1e, consumer purchase intention will have a mediating effect on their apparel purchase behavior and the variables of purchase antecedent such as consumers' attitude toward shopping apparel, emotional responses, and subjective norms; H3c, the level of consumers' apparel involvement will have a moderating effect on their apparel purchase intention and apparel purchase antecedents such as attitude toward shopping apparel, emotional responses, and social factors; and H4, the demographic variables of consumers in U.S. and Taiwan will be related to their attitude toward apparel shopping, emotional responses, subjective norms, apparel purchase intention and apparel behavior. No significant supports were found for H1d, the subjective norm will have a positive effect on the apparel purchase intention of Taiwan consumers; H2a, the subjective norm will have more influence on purchase intention of Taiwan consumers which are collectivist than on purchase intention of U.S. consumers which are individualist; H2c, consumer emotional responses while shopping will have more influence on purchase intention of U.S. consumers which are individualist than on purchase intention of Taiwan consumers which are collectivist; H3a, the need for cognition of consumers will have a moderating effect on their apparel purchase intention and apparel purchase antecedents such as attitude toward shopping apparel, emotional responses, and subjective norms; and H3b, the need for emotion of consumers will have a moderating effect on their apparel purchase intention and apparel purchase antecedents such as attitude toward shopping apparel, emotional responses, and subjective norms.

In the U.S., significant supports were found for H1a, the emotional responses while shopping for apparel will have an effect on their apparel purchase intention; H1d, the subjective norm will have a positive effect on the apparel purchase intention of consumers; and H2b, consumer attitudes toward apparel shopping will have more influence on purchase intention of Taiwan consumers which are collectivist than on purchase intention of U.S. consumers which are individualist. Partially significant supports were found for H1c, apparel shopping attitude factors of store ambience and services will have significant correlations to consumers' emotional responses; H1e, consumer purchase intention will have a mediating effect on their apparel purchase behavior and the variables of purchase antecedent such as consumers' attitude toward shopping apparel, emotional responses, and subjective norms; H3b, the need for emotion of consumers will have a moderating effect on their apparel purchase intention and apparel purchase antecedents such as attitude toward shopping apparel, emotional responses, and subjective norms; and H4, the demographic variables of consumers in U.S. and Taiwan will be related to their attitude toward apparel shopping, emotional responses, subjective norms, apparel purchase intention and apparel behavior.

No significant supports were found for H1b, the attitudes of consumers toward apparel shopping will have a positive effect on consumer' apparel purchase intention; H2a, the subjective norm will have more influence on purchase intention of Taiwan consumers which are collectivist than on purchase intention of U.S. consumers which are individualist was not supported; H2c, consumer emotional responses while shopping will have more influence on purchase intention of U.S. consumers which are individualist than on purchase intention of Taiwan consumers which are collectivist; and H3a, the need for cognition of consumers will have a moderating effect on their apparel purchase intention and apparel purchase antecedents such as attitude toward shopping apparel, emotional responses, and subjective norms; and H3c, the level of consumers' apparel involvement will have a moderating effect on their apparel purchase intention and apparel purchase antecedents such as attitude toward shopping apparel, emotional responses, and social factors.

Table 14   Summary of Hypotheses Findings for Taiwan and U.S.

Hypotheses
H1a*: The emotions when consumers are shopping apparel had an effect on consumers' apparel purchase intention in both Taiwan and U.S. consumers.
H1b**: The consumer attitude toward apparel shopping had a positive effect on consumers' apparel purchase intention in Taiwan consumers, but not in U.S. consumers.
H1c**: Apparel shopping attitudes factors in store ambience and services had significant correlations to consumers' emotional responses.
H1d**: The subjective norm had a positive effect on consumers' apparel purchase intention in U.S. consumers, but not in Taiwan consumers.
H1e*: Consumers' purchase intention had a mediating effect on apparel purchase behavior and purchase antecedent's variable (attitude, emotion, and subjective norm) in both U.S. and Taiwan consumers.
H2a: Subjective norm did not have more influence on Taiwanese (collectivist) consumers' purchase intention than on U.S. (individualist) consumers' purchase intention.
H2b*: Consumer attitudes toward apparel shopping had more influence on Taiwanese (collectivist) consumers' purchase intention than on U.S. (individualist) consumers' purchase intention.
H2c: The emotions when consumers are shopping did not have more influence on U.S. (individualist) consumers' purchase intention than on Taiwanese (collectivist) consumers' purchase intention.
H3a: The need for cognition did not have a moderating effect on apparel purchase intention and apparel purchase antecedents such as attitude, emotions, and subjective norm in both Taiwan and U.S. consumers.
H3b**: The need for emotion of consumers had a moderating effect on apparel purchase intention and the negative emotions when consumers are shopping in U.S. consumers, but not in Taiwan consumers.
H3c**: The apparel involvement of consumers had a moderating effect on apparel purchase intention and the positive emotions when consumers are shopping in Taiwan consumers, but not in U.S. consumers.
H4**: Consumers' demographic factor of gender was related to their attitude toward apparel shopping, emotional responses, subjective norm, apparel purchase intention and apparel behavior in both U.S. and Taiwanese consumers.

*Significant findings. **Partially significant findings

Chapter 5
Summary, Discussion, and Recommendations

The purpose of this dissertation was to examine the roles of consumers' emotional responses while shopping, consumer attitudes toward apparel shopping, subjective norms in social influence, individual differences and demographic factors for Taiwan and U.S. consumers' apparel purchase intentions and purchase behavior. Toward this end, in Taiwan significant support was found for H1a and H1b, and partially significant support was found for H1c, H1e, H2b, H3c, and H4. In the U.S., significant support was found for H1a and H1d, and partially significant support was found for H1c, H1e, H2b, H3b, and H4. This chapter summarizes demographics and hypotheses findings, discusses implications of findings, lists limitation and poses future research area.

Demographics

The demographics of this study revealed that the predominate consumer respondents for both countries were female (n = 248, 70% Taiwan; n = 362, 88.3% U.S.) undergraduate students (n = 337, 95.5% Taiwan; n = 388, 94.6% U.S.), between 18-24 years old (n = 321, 90.9% Taiwan; n = 385, 93.9% U.S.). There were 306 (74.6%) whites, 44 (10.7%) African-Americans, 44 (10.7%) Hispanics, and 16 (4%) Asians in the U.S. samples. In Taiwan, more than half of the respondents were living in the southern area (n = 193; 54.7%), followed by the northern area (n = 97; 27.5%), and the middle area (n = 63; 17.8%). More respondents reported either part-time or full time jobs in the U.S. (n = 217; 52.9%) than did Taiwan respondents (n = 93; 26.3%) who indicated they had either part-time or full time jobs. The average household income for U.S. samples is in the range of $70,000 to $84,999 US dollars, and the average household income in the Taiwan samples is in the range of $23,000 to $28,999 US dollars.

Findings for Emotional Responses While Consumers Are Shopping

The first objective was to investigate the relationships among apparel purchase behavior, apparel purchase intention and the variables of apparel purchase antecedents such as consumers' attitude toward shopping apparel, emotional responses, and social factors for U.S. and Taiwanese consumers. Hypothesis 1a, which states that the emotional responses while consumers are shopping for apparel have an effect on consumers' apparel purchase intention, was supported in both Taiwan and U.S. consumers. This finding supports the Triandis model, which treats attitude toward the act and social-normative considerations as determinants of intentions. However, departing from the TRA model, Triandis separates attitude toward the act into two terms: affect toward the act and the value of the perceived consequences of the act. Since we found consumers' emotional responses while shopping had an effect on consumer's apparel purchase intention, the Triandis model, which states that the attitude toward the act, social-normative, and affect toward the act are the determinants of consumer purchase intention (Triandis, 1982), was supported. The results of this research support that the Triandis Model can predict consumer apparel purchase intention more accurately than the TRA model. In this research we found that both positive and negative emotional responses while shopping had influence on consumer apparel purchase of Taiwan consumers, but only positive emotional responses had influence on consumer apparel purchase of U.S. consumers. To succeed in Taiwan, retailers need to not only create positive emotional responses while consumers are shopping, but also eliminate the negative emotional responses. Reasons why consumers listed negative emotional responses in Taiwan could be the store policy and service. In Taiwan, most stores do not have a return policy or the customer service area to deal with the customer complaints. In the U.S, customers can return their merchandise if they are not satisfied with the result, and there is always a place for consumers to go for customer issues; therefore, the negative emotional responses were not an issue for U.S. consumers in this study. Retailer in U.S. should try to create more positive emotional responses by having a pleasant store ambience and quality service, which were found to have positive relationships with positive emotional responses by consumers in this research study.

Hypothesis 1b, which states that the attitudes of consumers toward apparel shopping will have a positive effect on consumers' apparel purchase intention, was supported in Taiwan consumers, but not in U.S. consumers. It is interesting that four major factors were found in both U.S. and Taiwan's consumer attitude toward apparel shopping in this study. These factors were (1) product quality (good quality, variety, price, and brand); (2) employee service (sales personnel friendly, product knowledge, willingness to assist, and amount of employees); (3) ambience and interior/exterior design of the store (music, lighting, interior decoration and exterior architecture); and (4) convenience of shopping (parking, distance, travel time, crowding, walking space in store, and waiting time). Since the U.S. part of the data was collected in a mid-size town in Florida, some of the factors may not have contributed to the consumers' attitude toward apparel shopping. For instance, the item "parking in the shopping center," would not make a lot of sense in the town area since customers can always find a parking space except during the holiday reason, and the item "exterior architecture design" may not have an effect on consumers' apparel shopping attitude since consumers may have a limited number of choices in town. On the other hand, all items in this study were important to Taiwan consumers. Taiwan is an island about 160 kilometers off the southeast coast of mainland China with a size of 14,000 square miles and a population of 23 million. There can be more than 10 small shopping centers in a city. Due to the high level of competition, companies are trying different ways to attract their customers. Therefore, all facets in this study influence consumers' attitude toward apparel shopping in Taiwan.

Hypothesis 1d, which states that the subjective norm will have a positive effect on consumers' apparel purchase intention, was supported in U.S. consumers, but not in Taiwan consumers. The top three references U.S. respondents chose to listen were "friends," "parents," and "girl/boyfriend." In the U.S. data, 265 respondents chose "friend," 95 respondents chose "parents," and 79 respondents chose "boy/girlfriend" as their first preference when they purchase their apparel. On the other hand, even though data were collected in a southern city of Taiwan, students were from different areas (north = 97, middle = 63, and south =193) and exposed to all different media sources. The top three references Taiwan consumers will listen to are "friends," "girl/boyfriend," and "classmates." One hundred and seventy seven respondents chose "friend," 102 respondents chose "boy/girlfriend," and 52 respondents chose "classmates" as their first preference when they purchase their apparel. Both cultures chose "friend" as the most important influencer on apparel purchase decision.

Since the U.S. data were collected in a mid-size town in Florida, respondents may tend to listen to the norm more than people who live in a metropolitan city. Compared to people with less population density, people from an area of high population density would be exposed to more media, and have more choice of merchandise and retailer stores. This might be the reason why the subjective norm had a positive effect on consumers' apparel purchase intention in U.S. consumers, but not in Taiwan consumers. According to Pao (1996), in Taiwan Generation Y was born to a wealthy life; they don't have to worry about their life. Most of them are self-centered. They like fashionable merchandise, don't accept the traditional value or subject norms, like to enjoy life in food and apparel, are materialistic, and like the visual more than the textual. The result of the subjective norm for Taiwan consumers was consistent with Pao's (1996) analysis and Wang's (2005) studies that in the social influence of the subjective norm the Y generation will ask their friends' opinion about the apparel, but they will listen to themselves when making a purchase decision.

Hypothesis 1e, which states that consumers purchase intention will have a mediating effect on their apparel purchase behavior and the variables of purchase antecedent such as consumers' attitude toward shopping apparel, emotional responses, and subjective norms, was partially supported in both U.S. and Taiwan. In the U.S., data analysis using regression mediating, found all three equations were significant in the positive emotion and the beta weights dropped; therefore, partial mediation is present. In addition, the subjective norm has an insignificant beta weight in the third step; therefore, a complete mediation is present.

In Taiwan, since all three equations were significant in the positive emotions and negative emotions and the beta weights dropped, the partial mediation is present. Thus, partial support was provided for Hypothesis 1e; consumer purchase intention will have a mediating effect on purchase antecedents' variables (attitude, emotions when consumers are shopping, and subjective norm) and apparel purchase behavior. This result was consistent with Ajzen and Fishbein's (1980) Theory of Reasoned Action and Triandis's (1982) model that stated the purchase intention of consumer has a mediating effect on consumer purchase behavior.

Findings for Culture Difference

The second objective was to examine whether U.S. and Taiwan consumers exhibited any cultural difference in their apparel purchase antecedents and apparel purchase behavior. The Independent Samples T-test was utilized to examine the mean difference between Taiwan and U.S. consumers. Significant results were found in all research variables between Taiwan and U.S. consumers, except the need for cognition ($M_{U.S.}$ =3.28; M_{Taiwan} = 3.27, t = .33) and positive emotions when consumers are shopping ($M_{U.S.}$ = 2.77; M_{Taiwan} = 2.82, t = -.88). Hypothesis 2a, which states that the subjective norm will have more influence on the purchase intention of Taiwan consumers, which are collectivist, than on the purchase intention of U.S. consumers, which are individualist, was not supported since we found U.S. consumers had a higher mean score on subjective norm than Taiwan consumers ($M_{U.S.}$ = 12.02; M_{Taiwan} = 10.27), and the mean difference was significant between U.S. and Taiwan consumers ($t = 5.61, p < .001$). Hypothesis 2b, which states that consumer attitudes toward apparel shopping will have more influence on purchase intention of Taiwan consumers, which are collectivist, than on purchase intention of U.S. consumers, which are individualist, was supported since we found Taiwan consumers had a higher mean score on apparel shopping attitude than did U.S. consumers ($M_{U.S.} = 13.68$; $M_{Taiwan} = 14.79$) and the mean difference was significant between U.S. and Taiwan consumers ($t = -4.67$, $p < .001$).

The result of this research differs from Chang, Burns, and Noel (1996) and Casselman and Damhorst's (1991) findings that stated when apparel and other accessories were investigated most U.S. purchase intention was explained more by attitude toward purchasing than subjective norms. In this research, the apparel shopping attributes used were identical for U.S. and Taiwan consumers. Since consumer attitude toward apparel shopping was found significantly related to purchase intention in Taiwan but not in the U.S., it could be because some apparel attributes in the research were not to U.S. consumers as they were to Taiwanese consumers. In addition, the result was also the opposite of Chan and Lau's (1998) research of the Asian culture which found that Chinese consumers' intention to purchase traditional gold rings was influenced more by subjective norms than by attitude, and Lee and Green's (1991) research which found a similar result with Koreans' intentions to purchase sneakers. In this research, the subjective norm was not significant for consumers' apparel shopping intention in Taiwan consumers; it could be because of the different type of products in the research studies. In Chand and Lau's (1998) research, the traditional gold rings were used to examine the theory model. The traditional gold rings purchase behavior is an example of learning culture from our ancestors, and that may be the reason the subjective norms have influence to their purchase intention for this product. In Lee and Green's (1991) research, they used sneakers to examine the theory model. The sneakers were purchased most by the young generation, which often likes to be dressed the same and experiences peer group pressure. In our research, general apparel purchasing behavior was examined instead of a particular brand name apparel; therefore, the results indicated that the subjective norms had no relationship to consumer purchase intention in Taiwan.

Hypothesis 2c, which states that consumer emotional responses while shopping will have more influence on purchase intention of U.S. consumers, which are individualist, than on purchase intention of Taiwan consumers, which are collectivist, was not supported. In previous factor analysis it was found that the emotional responses while shopping had two directions, positive and negative emotions. Therefore, hypothesis 2c was analysized separately for positive emotions and negative emotions. There was no significant mean difference between the positive emotions when consumers are shopping between U.S. and Taiwan consumers ($M_{U.S.}$ = 2.77, M_{Taiwan} = 2.82, t = -.88). On the other hand, the negative emotions when consumers are shopping did have a significant mean difference between U.S. and Taiwan consumers ($M_{U.S.}$ = 1.36, M_{Taiwan} = 1.51, t = -4.11, p < .001). However, the result is not what was assumed. Taiwan consumers tended to have more negative emotions when they shopped than did U.S. consumers. Therefore, Hypothesis 2c, emotions when consumers are shopping will have more influence on U.S. consumers' purchase intention, was not supported.

Even though the emotional responses while consumers are shopping was not significantly different between Taiwan and U.S. consumers, the U.S. consumers did have a higher mean score in the need for emotion than did Taiwan consumers ($M_{U.S.}$ = 3.30, M_{Taiwan} = 1.54, t = 43.58, p < .001). This finding can help to explain expectations that consumers from an individualist country may have higher emotional expression than do consumers from a collectivist country. Additionally, U.S. consumers had lower apparel involvement than Taiwan consumers ($M_{U.S.}$ = 3.11, M_{Taiwan} = 3.75, t = -10.82, p < .001) and higher purchase intention ($M_{U.S.}$ = 3.48, M_{Taiwan} = 3.03, t = 8.91, p < .001). Regarding the higher apparel involvement for Taiwan consumers, it could be explained that Taiwan consumers may be exposed to more media, the average population density is higher, and the young generation enjoys shopping as a social activity. The U.S. data were collected in a southern city, the malls have less competition compared to Taiwan's shopping centers. It is possible that consumers who go to the mall may already have the intention to purchase something, instead of just enjoying the hedonic shopping experience.

Taiwan is an island about 160 kilometers off the southeast coast of mainland China with a size of 14,000 square miles and a population of 22.5 million. The average population density is 629 persons/ km2 in Taiwan, which is the second highest in the world. The highest density country is Bangladesh, with a population density of 1002 persons/ km2 and third is Korea with 487 persons/ km2. The population density in major cities of the northern and southern areas of Taiwan can reach 10,000 people per square kilometer (Statistical Yearbook of The Republic of China, 2003). Most respondents in this dissertation were younger in age. The younger generation can be separated into two groups: X generation (born between 1965 and 1976) and Y generation (born between 1977 and 1994). As previously discuss, in Taiwan Generation Y was born to a wealthy life, most of them are self-centered, they don't accept the traditional value, and like the visual more than the textual (Pao, 1996). In addition, in Wang's (2005) qualitative research, the younger respondents mentioned, if the sales person shows them fashion magazines featuring the dress at which they are looking, it will increase their purchase intention. This information may explain why Taiwan consumers' apparel purchase intention was influenced by their attitude toward apparel more than their subjective norms.

Findings for Individual Differences

The third objective was to examine the moderating effect of individual differences in the need for cognition, the need for emotion and apparel involvement on their apparel purchase intention. Hypothesis 3a, which states that the need for cognition of consumers will have a moderating effect on their apparel purchase intention and apparel purchase antecedents such as attitude toward shopping apparel, emotional responses, and social factors, was not supported for either Taiwan and U.S. consumers. Even though no moderating relationship was found in the need for cognition, an interesting positive relationship was found between need for cognition and apparel purchase intention in Taiwan consumers ($r = .19$, $p < .01$). This finding may help to explain the expectation that consumers from collectivist countries may have less emotional expression than consumers from individualist countries. Consumers in Taiwan, tend to like cognitive activities, such as thinking more than those activities involving emotional situations. This could be due to the educational system there as teachers always tell students to think carefully before making any decision, and that careful thinking will reduce mistakes. In addition, the non-return policy for apparel store may be the other reason causing consumers to think more carefully before they make the purchase.

Hypothesis 3b, which states that the need for emotion of consumers will have a moderating effect on their apparel purchase intention and apparel purchase antecedents such as attitude toward shopping apparel, emotional responses, and social factors, was supported in U.S. consumers, but not in Taiwan consumers. In the U.S., respondents who had a high score for the need for emotion and a low score for negative emotions when they were shopping held the highest level of purchase intention. On the other hand, the lowest level of consumer purchase intention was held by those consumers who had a high score for the need for emotion and a high score for negative emotions while shopping. This research found that U.S. consumers who had a low need for emotion did not have a huge difference in their purchase intention, with either the low or high negative emotional responses while shopping. However, this research found that U.S. consumers who had a high need for emotion and low negative emotional responses while shopping tended to have the highest purchase intention, and consumers who had a high need for emotion and high negative emotional responses while shopping tended to have the lowest purchase intention. Retailers should pay more attention to consumers who have a high need for emotion and try to minimize on eliminate their negative emotional responses. In this way, consumers' purchase intention will increase which in turn will increase business sales.

Hypothesis 3c, which states that the level of consumers' apparel involvement will have a moderating effect on their apparel purchase intention and apparel purchase antecedents such as attitude toward shopping apparel, emotional responses, and social factors, was supported in Taiwan consumers, but not U.S. consumers. In Taiwan, respondents who have a low score in apparel involvement and a low score for positive emotions when they are shopping held the highest level of purchase intention. On the other hand, the lowest level of consumer purchase intention was held by those consumers who had a low score in apparel involvement and a high score for positive emotions while shopping in Taiwan. As expected, this research found that the Taiwan consumer who had high apparel involvement and high positive emotional responses while shopping tended to have higher apparel purchase intention than consumers who had high apparel involvement and low positive emotional responses while shopping. More interesting, this research found the Taiwan consumers who had low apparel involvement and low positive emotional responses tended to have the highest apparel purchase intention, and consumers who had low apparel involvement and high positive emotional responses while shopping tended to have the lowest apparel purchase intention. Marketers need to be careful while they try to create positive emotions to the low apparel involvement group of consumers. While introducing positive emotional factors in the stores, retailers should have different strategies for consumers' with different levels of apparel involvement.

Findings for Demographic

The fourth objective is to examine the demographic factors of age, gender, occupation, income, and education level. The data were collected from university students, descriptive statistic show that over 90% of the respondents were undergraduate students 18-24 years old. Therefore, these two variables were not included in multivariate analysis of variances (*MANOVAs*). Hypothesis 4 was partially supported for both U.S. and Taiwan consumers. In U.S. consumers, gender was significantly related to consumers apparel purchase antecedent variables ($F = 2.60$, $p < .05$, observed power $= .92$). More specifically, gender was significantly related to the individual difference in need for emotion ($F = 5.11, p < .05$), apparel involvement ($F = 5.04$, $p < .05$), and the negative emotions when consumers are shopping ($F = 4.20$, $p < .05$). The results are consistent with bivariate correlations analysis which found female consumers tended to have higher scores in the need for emotion ($r = .19$, $p < .01$), higher negative emotions when they are shopping ($r = .11$, $p < .01$) and higher apparel involvement ($r = .26$, $p < .01$) than did male consumers.

In Taiwan consumers, gender was significantly related to consumers' apparel purchase antecedent variables ($F = 3.48$, $p < .01$, observed power = .98). More specifically, gender was significantly related to the individual difference in apparel involvement ($F = 7.18$, $p < .01$), subjective norm ($F = 4.50$, $p < .01$), and apparel purchase intention ($F = 4.73$, $p < .05$).The results are consistent with bivariate correlations analysis which found female consumers tended to have more apparel involvement ($r = .20$, $p < .01$), higher subjective norm ($r = .20$, $p < .01$), and higher apparel purchase intention ($r = .12$, $p < .05$). According to Freedman (1986), femininity and beauty cannot be separated. In most cultures, women are expected to be concerned with fashion and beauty. In this research, we found that both the U.S. and Taiwan female consumers had higher apparel involvement levels than did male consumers. The findings of this research were also consistent with previous literature which has shown that women have a higher concern for clothing and fashion consciousness (Solomon & Schopler, 1982).

Limitations

Data were collected from two southern Universities in Taiwan and one southern University in the U.S. to represent Eastern and Western cultures. However, consumers who live in other cities or countries in the East and West might have different perspectives from the data which were collected in Taiwan and the U.S. Another limitation for this sample was the lack of a random sample. The statistical conclusions of the inferential statistics should be taken with caution. Future research should strive to attain a random sample, and use non-parametric statistics that do not have as many rigid assumptions. Additionally, this study only examined the product category of consumers' apparel purchase intention related to consumers' emotional response, apparel shopping attributes, subjective norms, personal differences in the need for cognition, emotion, and apparel involvement constructs. Other product categories should use the results of this study with caution. Also, there are some constructs that may have influence on consumers' apparel purchase behavior which were not included in this study. For instance, the situational factors for out-of-stock merchandise, time pressure, and consumer subjective knowledge in clothing may have influence on consumers' apparel purchase behavior also. The apparel shopping attribute items which were selected for this study may not covered all the factors of the apparel shopping attributes.

Based on different data collection methods, there would have different disadvantages and advantages. In this study data were collected via internet questionnaire by consumers' self-administered responses. This method can reduce human mistakes at the data entry stage, but on the other hand it's hard to measure the response rate, and the consumer may fill out the questionnaire arbitrarily. Generally, the results generated from this study should be interpreted carefully with consideration to limitations.

Future Research

In future studies, apparel shopping attribute items will need more careful examination and could include additional attributes. In this study, the apparel shopping attribute items which were used to calculate consumer attitude toward apparel shopping were not significant to consumer apparel purchase intention in the U.S. data. In future research, a deep qualitative interview could be done in advance to determine the importance of apparel shopping attributes. An attribute items pool could be given in a pre-test to get respondents' input on attributes that will influence their apparel shopping attitude. Secondly, this study only examined the factors of emotional responses, consumer attitude, and subjective norm that would influence consumer purchase intention for the Triandis model. In the Triandis model, consumer purchase behavior is not only determined by consumer purchase intention, but also by consumer habit and facilitating conditions. For instance, facilitating condition differences in a department store, specialty store, and prestige brand store may have a relationship to consumer purchase behavior. In the future, it will be interesting to examine all the factors in the Triandis model.

Third, the research model can be examined by using different statistical analysis such as structural equation modeling (SEM). SEM allows researchers in the social sciences, management sciences, behavioral sciences and other fields to empirically assess their theories. These theories are usually formulated as theoretical models for observed and unobservable variables. If data are collected for the observed variables of the theoretical model, the *LISREL* program could be used to fit the model to the data. The *LISREL* program could assist the researcher in viewing the path loadings of the overall model at once. In addition, the *LISREL* program could assist with comparison between samples with all the variables in the model at the same time.

Furthermore, future research can be done regarding emotional expression in the consumers' satisfaction responses. Satisfaction was defined as the consumer's fulfillment response (Oliver, 1997). Few studies stated and used consumers' emotional responses while shopping to measure customers' satisfactions, however, the question of whether satisfaction is an emotion has not been answered. In addition, consumers' desire may need to be included in the future research about purchase behavior, For instance, consumers desiring hedonic fulfillment (shopping experience of relaxing and enjoyment) would expect different attributes than the functional fulfillment apparel shopper (a rational buying decision, as buying a business suit for an interview). At last, it would be interesting to examine the individual differences in materialism and hedonic shopping value which are a trend now in the young generation. Moreover, comparison of different generations' value and apparel attitude can be done in future research. Also, random sample and consumer samples from other countries, which represent Western and Eastern culture could be examined.

Appendix A. Online Cover Page

Appendix B. Online Cover Letter English Edition

Dear Consumers:

Since there is more apparel retailing across boundary lines of different countries, we would like to investigate several factors that may have an influence on your final purchase decision or purchase intention of apparel. This study is part of my PhD dissertation and will investigate the following ideas: your attitudes toward apparel shopping, your feeling about the apparel shopping trip, the people who influence your apparel purchase, individual differences, and demographic factors. The results of this study will be shared with retailers in both Taiwan and U.S. to better understand your retail environment by educating present and future retailers on the needs and wants of their customers. Your participation in this survey will be greatly appreciated.

The questionnaire will take only 15 – 30 minutes to complete, and your participation is very important to the success of our research. There is no risk to you, and the questionnaire is anonymous. Identification e-mail will be used only for convenience purposes to organize the raw data. The results of this study may be published, but your name will not be known. Participants in this study need to be 18 years of age or older to meet university guidelines so by participating in the study you're verifying that you're 18 years or older. Again, I appreciate your patience and willingness in this research project.

We look forward to your response and comments concerning this project. If you have any questions, please feel free to contact Dr. Jeanne Heitmeyer who is my major professor at 850-644-5578, jheitmey@mailer.fsu.edu in U.S. or Yun Wang at 07-211-5058 [in Taiwan from 05/20/2004 to 07/20/2005], yunw@hotmail.com in Taiwan.

Please enter your E-mail
address   [send]

Appendix C. Online Survey For English Edition

QUESTIONNAIRE

Please **complete Part I of the questionnaire today.** Then complete Part II right before you shop for apparel. Part III of the questionnaire will need to be filled out after your apparel-shopping trip. To continue your answer of each part of questionnaire you will need to **re-enter your e-mail address** at the beginning, and please answer the questionnaire to reflect your feelings about your shopping trip. Thanks for helping me by filling out this questionnaire.

Part I - a.

Please read each statement and check the circle of the most appropriate number that expresses your feelings. For example: you strongly disagree (1)/ strongly agree (5) "I prefer to keep my feelings hidden.?

	Strongly Disagree	Disagree	Neutral	Agree	Strongly Agree
1. I try to anticipate and avoid situations where there is a likely chance of my getting emotionally involved.	○1	○2	○3	○4	○5
2. Experiencing strong emotions is not something I enjoy very much.	○1	○2	○3	○4	○5
3. I would rather be in a situation where I experience little emotion than get me emotionally involved.	○1	○2	○3	○4	○5
4. I like to be unemotional in emotional situations.	○1	○2	○3	○4	○5
5. I find little satisfaction in experiencing strong emotions.	○1	○2	○3	○4	○5
6. I prefer to keep my feelings hidden.	○1	○2	○3	○4	○5
7. I feel relief rather than fulfillment after experiencing a situation that was very emotional.	○1	○2	○3	○4	○5
8. I prefer to ignore the emotional aspects of situations rather than getting involved in them.	○1	○2	○3	○4	○5
9. I don't look forward to being in situations that others have found to be emotional.	○1	○2	○3	○4	○5
10. I have tried to answer all of these questions honestly and accurately	○1	○2	○3	○4	○5
11. More often than not, making decisions based on emotions just leads to more errors.	○1	○2	○3	○4	○5
12. I don't like to have the responsibility of handling a situation that is emotional in nature.	○1	○2	○3	○4	○5
13. I look forward to situations that I know are less emotionally involving.	○1	○2	○3	○4	○5

Part I - b.

This section includes questions related to apparel shopping attributes you consider important when you shop for an apparel product. On a scale of 1 (*Very unimportant*) to 5 (*very important*), please indicate how important the following qualities are when you shop for an apparel product.

For example: Ample parking is Very unimportant (1) / Very Important (5) to me when I shop for apparel.

Items/ Scales	Very unimportant	-	Neutral	-	Very Important
1. Ample parking	○1	○2	○3	○4	○5
2. Short walking distance between parking and store	○1	○2	○3	○4	○5
3. Short travel time or distance between your house and shopping center	○1	○2	○3	○4	○5
4. Low amount of crowding in stores (i.e. short check-out lines)	○1	○2	○3	○4	○5
5. Ample walking space between merchandise	○1	○2	○3	○4	○5
6. Good quality apparel merchandise	○1	○2	○3	○4	○5
7. Variety of apparel merchandise	○1	○2	○3	○4	○5
8. Reasonable price ranges of apparel	○1	○2	○3	○4	○5
9. Brand selection	○1	○2	○3	○4	○5
10. Music selection that I like	○1	○2	○3	○4	○5
11. Appropriate sound level of music	○1	○2	○3	○4	○5
12. Sufficient lighting	○1	○2	○3	○4	○5
13. Attractive interior decoration	○1	○2	○3	○4	○5
14. Attractive exterior architecture	○1	○2	○3	○4	○5
15. Sales personnel are not giving me pressure to buy	○1	○2	○3	○4	○5
16. Sales personnel have sufficient product knowledge	○1	○2	○3	○4	○5
17. Sales personnel are willing to assist you	○1	○2	○3	○4	○5
18. Appropriate number of sales personnel in store	○1	○2	○3	○4	○5

Part I - c.

On a scale of 1 to 5, please circle the number that best reflects your feelings of apparel.

Apparel is:

1. Unimportant to me	○1	-	○2	-	○3	-	○4	-	○5	Important to me
2. Of concern to me	○1	-	○2	-	○3	-	○4	-	○5	Of no concern
3. Means nothing to me	○1	-	○2	-	○3	-	○4	-	○5	Means a lot to me
4. Does not matter to me	○1	-	○2	-	○3	-	○4	-	○5	Matters to me
5. Significant to me	○1	-	○2	-	○3	-	○4	-	○5	Insignificant to me

Part I - d.

Please read the following statement and circle the most appropriate number that expresses your thoughts from 1 (*completely false*) to 5 (*completely true*). For instance, "I would prefer complex rather than simple problems.?If you feel the statement was false, then you will circle the number ??which indicates "False? for the statement.

Items/ scales	Completely false	False	Neutral	True	Completely true
1. I would prefer complex rather than simple problems.	1	2	3	4	5
2. I like to have the responsibility of handling a situation that requires a lot of thinking.	1	2	3	4	5
3. Thinking is not my idea of fun.	1	2	3	4	5
4. I would rather do something that requires little thought than something that is sure to challenge my thinking abilities.	1	2	3	4	5
5. I try to and avoid situations where there is a likely chance I will have to think in depth about something.	1	2	3	4	5
6. I find satisfaction in deliberating hard and for long hours.	1	2	3	4	5
7. I only think as hard as I have to.	1	2	3	4	5
8. I prefer to think about small, daily projects rather than long-term ones.	1	2	3	4	5
9. I like tasks that require little thought once I've learned them.	1	2	3	4	5
10. The idea of relying on thought to make my way to the top appeals to me.	1	2	3	4	5
11. I really enjoy a task that involves coming up with new solutions to problems.	1	2	3	4	5
12. Learning new ways to think doesn't excite me very much.	1	2	3	4	5
13. I prefer my life to be filled with puzzles that I must solve.	1	2	3	4	5
14. The notion of thinking abstractly is appealing to me.	1	2	3	4	5
15. I would prefer a task that is intellectual, difficult, and important to one that is somewhat important but does not require much thought.	1	2	3	4	5
16. I feel relief rather than satisfaction after completing a task that required a lot of mental effort.	1	2	3	4	5
17. It's enough for me that something gets the job done; I don't care how or why it works.	1	2	3	4	5
18. I usually end up deliberating about issues even when they do not affect me personally.	1	2	3	4	5

Send   Reset

Part II.
Please complete the following questions before you go shopping for apparel

1. Please indicate your apparel purchase intention for today's shopping trip.

○ To browse   ○ To buy a specific item   ○ Both

2. Please circle the possibility you will buy apparel when you go shopping today

○ 0%   ○ 25%   ○ 50%   ○ 75%   ○ 100%

3. Please circle the number that mostly indicates to your apparel purchase intention for today's shopping trip.

a. Unlikely	○ 1 -	○ 2 -	○ 3 -	○ 4 -	○ 5	Likely
b. Impossible	○ 1 -	○ 2 -	○ 3 -	○ 4 -	○ 5	Possible
c. Probable	○ 1 -	○ 2 -	○ 3 -	○ 4 -	○ 5	Improbable
d. Uncertain	○ 1 -	○ 2 -	○ 3 -	○ 4 -	○ 5	Certain

Send   Reset

Enjoy your shopping and please don't forget the fill out the rest of the questionnaire after you come back!!!☺ ☺ ☺

Part III. Please complete these questions AFTER your shopping trip for apparel

---

Part III - a.

1. Did you make any apparel purchase today?　○ Yes　○ No
2. How many pieces did you buy today?　○ 0　○ 1　○ 2　○ 3　○ 4　○ 5　○ 5+
3. Did you buy any **tops** today?

○ Yes, I bought some ☐ shirts & blouses, ☐ T-shirts, ☐ sweaters, or ☐ vests & jackets

○ No, I bought some ☐ skirt, ☐ shorts, ☐ dresses, or ☐ jeans & trousers

○ No, I didn't buy anything today.

Part III - b.

This section includes questions related to the apparel shopping you just made. Please **consider the apparel shopping attributes that impacted your apparel purchase or nonpurchase.** On a scale of 1 to 5, with 1 being "very unlikely?and 5 being "very likely? indicate how likely you think it is that the following apparel shopping attributes impacted your purchase decision.

For example: It is Very Unlikely (1) / Very Likely (5) that I would find ample parking while I shopped for the apparel today.

Items/ Scales	Very Unlikely	-	Neutral	-	Very Likely
1. Ample parking	○ 1	○ 2	○ 3	○ 4	○ 5
2. Short walking distance between parking and store	○ 1	○ 2	○ 3	○ 4	○ 5
3. Short travel time or distance between your house and shopping center	○ 1	○ 2	○ 3	○ 4	○ 5
4. Low amount of crowding in stores (i.e. short check-out lines)	○ 1	○ 2	○ 3	○ 4	○ 5
5. Ample walking space between merchandise	○ 1	○ 2	○ 3	○ 4	○ 5
6. Good quality apparel merchandise	○ 1	○ 2	○ 3	○ 4	○ 5
7. Variety of apparel merchandise	○ 1	○ 2	○ 3	○ 4	○ 5
8. Reasonable price ranges of apparel	○ 1	○ 2	○ 3	○ 4	○ 5
9. Brand selection	○ 1	○ 2	○ 3	○ 4	○ 5
10. Music selection that I like	○ 1	○ 2	○ 3	○ 4	○ 5
11. Appropriate sound level of music	○ 1	○ 2	○ 3	○ 4	○ 5
12. Sufficient lighting	○ 1	○ 2	○ 3	○ 4	○ 5
13. Attractive interior decoration	○ 1	○ 2	○ 3	○ 4	○ 5
14. Attractive exterior architecture	○ 1	○ 2	○ 3	○ 4	○ 5
15. If you read this item do not respond to it	○ 1	○ 2	○ 3	○ 4	○ 5
16. Sales personnel are not giving me pressure to buy	○ 1	○ 2	○ 3	○ 4	○ 5
17. Sales personnel have sufficient product knowledge	○ 1	○ 2	○ 3	○ 4	○ 5
18. Sales personnel are willing to assist you	○ 1	○ 2	○ 3	○ 4	○ 5
19. Appropriate number of sales personnel in store	○ 1	○ 2	○ 3	○ 4	○ 5

Part III - c.

Please answer the following questions by thinking about how you felt while shopping for your apparel today by using a 5-point scale from 1 -*not at all*, 2 -*a little*, 3 - *moderately*, 4- *strongly*, to 5 *very strongly.*

For example: I felt Not at all (1) / Very strongly (5) of anger when I shopped today!!

Emotion items	Not at all	A little	Moderate	Strongly	Very strongly
1. Anger (frustrated, angry, and irritated)	○1	○2	○3	○4	○5
2. Discontent (unfulfilled and discontented)	○1	○2	○3	○4	○5
3. Worry (nervous, worried, and tense)	○1	○2	○3	○4	○5
4. Sadness (depressed, sad, and miserable)	○1	○2	○3	○4	○5
5. Fear (scared, afraid, and panicky)	○1	○2	○3	○4	○5
6. Shame (embarrassed, ashamed, humiliated)	○1	○2	○3	○4	○5
7. Envy (envious and jealous)	○1	○2	○3	○4	○5
8. Loneliness (lonely and homesick)	○1	○2	○3	○4	○5
9. Romantic (sexy, romantic, and passionate)	○1	○2	○3	○4	○5
10. Love (sentimental and warm hearted)	○1	○2	○3	○4	○5
11. Peacefulness (calm and peaceful)	○1	○2	○3	○4	○5
12. Contentment (content and fulfilled)	○1	○2	○3	○4	○5
13. Optimism (optimistic, encouraged, hopeful)	○1	○2	○3	○4	○5
14. Joy (happy, pleased and joyful)	○1	○2	○3	○4	○5
15. Excitement (excited, thrilled, enthusiastic)	○1	○2	○3	○4	○5
16. Surprise (surprised, amazed and astonished)	○1	○2	○3	○4	○5

Part III - d.

Please rank **the three most important people** you seek for advice when purchase apparel (The number 1 indicates the most important followed by 2 and3.)

Mother / Father	Brothers / Sisters	Wife / Husband	Friends
Girlfriend / Boyfriend	Classmate	Colleague	Sales Assistant
Others	(please write down)		

Part III - e.

Please circle the answer **you believe** most closely reflects **how much others support** your apparel purchasing behavior. You will indicate your answer by a five-point scale from 1 (*not at all*) to 5 (*strongly support*).

1. Do your family members support your apparel purchasing?

   ○ 1.not at all   ○ 2.very little   ○ 3.little   ○ 4.support   ○ 5.strongly support

2. Do your friends (including boy/girlfriend) support your apparel purchasing behavior?

   ○ 1.not at all   ○ 2.very little   ○ 3.little   ○ 4.support   ○ 5.strongly support

3. Do salespersons support your apparel purchasing behavior?

   ○ 1.not at all   ○ 2.very little   ○ 3.little   ○ 4.support   ○ 5.strongly support

Please indicate your **motivation to comply** with the thoughts of others in your apparel purchasing behavior by a-five point scale from 1 (*not at all*) to 5 (*very often*).

4. How often do your family members?opinions influence your apparel purchase decisions?

   ○ 1.not at all   ○ 2.very little   ○ 3.sometimes   ○ 4.often   ○ 5.very often

5. How often do your friends?opinions influence your apparel purchase decisions?

   ○ 1.not at all   ○ 2.very little   ○ 3.sometimes   ○ 4.often   ○ 5.very often

6. How often do salespersons?opinions influence your apparel purchase decisions?

   ○ 1.not at all   ○ 2.very little   ○ 3.sometimes   ○ 4.often   ○ 5.very often

---

Send   Reset

Demographics

1. Are you? ○ Male ○ Female

2. Are you an ○ undergraduate student ○ graduate student

3. What ethnic group do you consider yourself to be a member of?

○ White/Caucasian ○ African American/Black

○ Hispanic/Latino

○ Asian American/Asian ○ American Indian

○ Other

4. Are you: ○ Unemployed ○ Employed

☐ Employed Part Time – Your occupation

is

☐ Employed Full Time – Your occupation

is

5. What is your age category?

○ 18-24 ○ 25-31 ○ 32-38 ○ 39-45 ○ 46-
52 ○ 53-59 ○ 60+

6. Please check the category that best represents your family's annual household income before taxes.

○ Less than $ 9,999 ○ $10,000 -
$24,999 ○ $25,000 - $39,999

○ $40,000 - $54,999 ○ $55,000 -
$69,999 ○ $70,000 - $84,999

○ $85,000 - $99,999 ○ $100,000 -
$114,999 ○ More than $115,000

If you have any additional comments regarding this study, please write it down after you finish these questions.

Send   Reset

Appendix D. Online Cover Letter For Chinese Edition

　　您好！我是美國佛羅里達州立大學服飾經營系的博士班研究生，此研究為我的博士論文，主要是針對消費者對購買服飾的態度，購買時情緒、個人特性不同、社會團體之影響、及人口經濟之因素來預測消費者購買服飾之行為。研究結果將幫助服飾廠商多認識、多了解消費者之需求，進而改進服務品質與產品。

　　填寫問卷者必須年滿18歲，填寫之問卷以無記名方式，前後所需時間約15分鐘。此問卷僅供學術研究資料分析不會移作他用，請放心作答。非常感謝你的熱心協助，如果你有任何問題請來電 07-2115058；0952-484-888 或 e-mail 給我yunw@hotmail.com

再次感謝您的幫助！

請輸入您的 E-
mail　　　　　　　　　　　　　　　送出

Appendix E. Online Survey For Chinese Edition

問卷內容

本問卷共有三部份。請現在開始並完成第一部份的問卷，然後在你去逛街以前填寫第二部分的問卷。第三部分的問卷請在逛完街回家後立即填寫。

在完成第一部份問卷離開後，如要繼續填寫問卷，你只需在首頁重新輸入你上次輸入的e-mail就可以繼續下一部份的問卷了。 謝謝你的幫忙。

Part - I - a

在閱讀完下列敘述說明後，請圈選最適當的數字來表達你對情感需求的認同程度。 "1"代表非常不同意, "5"代表非常同意

	非常不同意	不同意	中立的	同意	非常同意
1. 我試著去避免自己有可能受到情緒影響的情境	○1	○2	○3	○4	○5
2. 體驗強烈的情緒並不是我很喜歡的事	○1	○2	○3	○4	○5
3. 我比較喜歡在很少情緒化的情境，而非在情緒化的情境	○1	○2	○3	○4	○5
4. 我喜歡在情緒化的情境中保持理性	○1	○2	○3	○4	○5
5. 在強烈的情緒體驗中，我極少感到滿足	○1	○2	○3	○4	○5
6. 我寧願隱藏我的感覺	○1	○2	○3	○4	○5
7. 在經歷非常情緒化的情境後，我覺得鬆了一口氣，而非有成就感	○1	○2	○3	○4	○5
8. 我寧願選擇忽略情緒的感覺，而非深入其境.	○1	○2	○3	○4	○5
9. 我不想把自己涉入其他人認為是情緒化的情境	○1	○2	○3	○4	○5
10. 我試著誠實且正確的回答所有的問題	○1	○2	○3	○4	○5
11. 依賴情緒做決定，常常會帶來更多的錯誤	○1	○2	○3	○4	○5
12. 我不喜歡負責處理含有情緒性質的工作	○1	○2	○3	○4	○5
13. 我期待較少涉及情緒的情境	○1	○2	○3	○4	○5

Part - I - b

下列是有關你在購買服飾時認為是主要屬性的問題。請用 1 至 5 的數字來表示你的看法
"1" 表示非常不重要，"5" 表示非常重要

	非常不重要	—	普通	—	非常重要
1. 有足夠的停車位	○1	○2	○3	○4	○5
2. 停車地點與商店間的步行距離不遠	○1	○2	○3	○4	○5
3. 從住家到商店街的時間短或距離近	○1	○2	○3	○4	○5
4. 商店內不擁擠/等待結帳的人不多	○1	○2	○3	○4	○5
5. 商店內的走道空間寬敞	○1	○2	○3	○4	○5
6. 服飾商品品質優良	○1	○2	○3	○4	○5
7. 服飾商品種類繁多	○1	○2	○3	○4	○5
8. 服飾商品價格合理	○1	○2	○3	○4	○5
9. 品牌選擇多	○1	○2	○3	○4	○5
10. 店內的音樂是我喜歡的	○1	○2	○3	○4	○5
11. 店內音樂的音量適當	○1	○2	○3	○4	○5
12. 店內燈光充足	○1	○2	○3	○4	○5
13. 店內的佈置裝潢有吸引力	○1	○2	○3	○4	○5
14. 建築外觀有吸引力	○1	○2	○3	○4	○5
15. 銷售人員不會給我購買的壓力	○1	○2	○3	○4	○5
16. 銷售人員有足夠的產品知識	○1	○2	○3	○4	○5
17. 銷售人員願意幫忙	○1	○2	○3	○4	○5
18. 店內銷售人員的數量適當	○1	○2	○3	○4	○5

Part - I - c

請依照你個人對服裝的感覺，圈選最靠近你想法的數字

你認為服裝：

1. 對我不重要	○1 —	○2 —	○3 —	○4 —	○5	對我重要
2. 是我關切的	○1 —	○2 —	○3 —	○4 —	○5	是我不關切的
3. 對我沒意義	○1 —	○2 —	○3 —	○4 —	○5	對我有重要意義
4. 我不在乎	○1 —	○2 —	○3 —	○4 —	○5	我在乎
5. 對我意味深長的	○1 —	○2 —	○3 —	○4 —	○5	對我微不足道的

Part - I - d

在下列問題中，請圈選最適當的數字，來表示你的想法，"1" 代表完全錯誤, "5" 代表完全正確

	完全錯誤	錯誤	中立的	正確	完全正確
1. 我喜歡複雜而非簡單的問題	○1	○2	○3	○4	○5
2. 我喜歡負責處理需要深入思考的情境	○1	○2	○3	○4	○5
3. 我認為思考不好玩	○1	○2	○3	○4	○5
4. 我喜歡去做只需要花很少心思的工作，而非挑戰腦力的事	○1	○2	○3	○4	○5
5. 我會試著去避免有可能需要深入思考的情境	○1	○2	○3	○4	○5
6. 我能從長時間的深思熟慮中找到滿足	○1	○2	○3	○4	○5
7. 我只做必要的思考	○1	○2	○3	○4	○5
8. 我較喜歡去想日常的小事，而非長期的事情	○1	○2	○3	○4	○5
9. 我喜歡一旦學會之後只需很少思考的工作	○1	○2	○3	○4	○5
10. 依賴思考去走向高峰的想法很吸引我	○1	○2	○3	○4	○5
11. 我真的喜歡那種可找出新的解決方式的工作	○1	○2	○3	○4	○5
12. 學習新的思考方式不會讓我感到非常鼓舞	○1	○2	○3	○4	○5
13. 我喜歡我的生命中充滿了必須解決的難題	○1	○2	○3	○4	○5
14. 抽象思考的想法會吸引我	○1	○2	○3	○4	○5
15. 我比較喜歡有智慧、困難且重要的工作，而非有些重要但不需太多思考的工作	○1	○2	○3	○4	○5
16. 當我完成一件需要很多心智的工作，我覺得輕鬆而不是滿足感	○1	○2	○3	○4	○5
17. 對我而言工作做完就夠了，我不在乎它如何有效或為何而做	○1	○2	○3	○4	○5
18. 既使是不影響我個人的問題，我通常也會用心去思考	○1	○2	○3	○4	○5

確定送出　重新填寫

第二部分:

1. 請勾選你今天逛街購買服飾的意圖

○ 沒事逛逛 　　　　　　　　○ 去購買特定的東西　　　○ 兩者皆是

2. 請圈選你今天去逛街時購買服飾的可能性

　　○ 0%　　　○ 25%　　　○ 50%
　　　　○ 75%　　　○ 100%

3. 請圈選最靠近你今天逛街購買服飾意圖的數字

a. 不會發生	○1	—	○2	—	○3	—	○4	—	○5	會發生
b. 不可能的	○1	—	○2	—	○3	—	○4	—	○5	有可能的
c. 有機會	○1	—	○2	—	○3	—	○4	—	○5	沒有機會
d. 不確定的	○1	—	○2	—	○3	—	○4	—	○5	確定的

[確定送出]　[重新填寫]

你已經完成第二部分的問卷了,請別忘了在逛街回來後,繼續完成剩下的問卷!!

第三部分: 請在<u>逛街回來後</u>繼續完成此部份問卷

Part III - a

1. 請問你今天有購買任何服飾嗎?　　○有　　○沒有

2. 你今天共買了幾件服飾?　　○0　○1　○2　○3　○4　○5　○5+

3. 請問你有買購買任何上衣嗎?

　　○有。我買了 □襯衫 □T恤 □套頭衫 □背心/夾克

　　○沒有。我買了 □裙子 □短褲 □洋裝 □牛仔褲/長褲

　　○沒有,我今天沒有購買任何服飾。

Part III - b

請依下列18項購買服飾時的屬性,由1至5的標準,來評估影響你今天購買的服飾的適當性。 請直接圈選最適當的答案. "1" 表示非常不恰當,不合適的, "5" 表示非常恰當,合適。

	非常不恰當	—	中立	—	非常恰當
1. 有足夠的停車位	○1	○2	○3	○4	○5
2. 停車地點與商店間的步行距離不遠	○1	○2	○3	○4	○5
3. 從住家到商店街的時間短或距離不遠	○1	○2	○3	○4	○5
4. 商店內不擁擠/等待結帳的人不多	○1	○2	○3	○4	○5
5. 商店內有足夠的走道空間	○1	○2	○3	○4	○5
6. 服飾商品品質優良	○1	○2	○3	○4	○5
7. 服飾商品種類繁多	○1	○2	○3	○4	○5
8. 服飾商品價格合理	○1	○2	○3	○4	○5
9. 品牌選擇多	○1	○2	○3	○4	○5
10. 我喜歡店內的音樂	○1	○2	○3	○4	○5
11. 店內音樂的音量適當	○1	○2	○3	○4	○5
12. 店內燈光充足	○1	○2	○3	○4	○5
13. 店內的佈置裝潢有吸引力	○1	○2	○3	○4	○5
14. 商店街建築外觀有吸引力	○1	○2	○3	○4	○5
15. 如果你看到這個題目請跳過不要作答	○1	○2	○3	○4	○5
16. 銷售人員不會給我購買的壓力	○1	○2	○3	○4	○5
17. 銷售人員有足夠的產品知識	○1	○2	○3	○4	○5
18. 銷售人員願意幫忙	○1	○2	○3	○4	○5
19. 店內銷售人員的數量適當	○1	○2	○3	○4	○5

Part III - c

在你開始填寫此部份問題前，請回想一下你今天在逛街時購買服飾時的感覺，然後直接圈選最適當的答案。例如 "1" 表示完全沒感覺，"5" 表示有非常強烈的感覺

	完全沒感覺	一點點	適中的	強烈的	非常強烈感覺
1. 生氣、沮喪、憤怒、受刺激的	○1	○2	○3	○4	○5
2. 不滿足的、不滿意的	○1	○2	○3	○4	○5
3. 擔心的、緊張的、緊繃的	○1	○2	○3	○4	○5
4. 悲傷的、難過的、壓抑的	○1	○2	○3	○4	○5
5. 害怕的、恐懼的、丟臉的	○1	○2	○3	○4	○5
6. 困窘的、羞恥的	○1	○2	○3	○4	○5
7. 忌妒的、羨慕的	○1	○2	○3	○4	○5
8. 寂寞的、孤單的、想家的	○1	○2	○3	○4	○5
9. 羅曼蒂克的、熱情的、性感的	○1	○2	○3	○4	○5
10. 愛的、溫暖的、情感的	○1	○2	○3	○4	○5
11. 和平的、冷靜的、平靜的	○1	○2	○3	○4	○5
12. 滿意的、滿足的	○1	○2	○3	○4	○5
13. 樂觀的、有希望的、受鼓舞的	○1	○2	○3	○4	○5
14. 喜悅的、快樂的、高興的	○1	○2	○3	○4	○5
15. 興奮的、熱誠的	○1	○2	○3	○4	○5
16. 驚訝的、驚奇的	○1	○2	○3	○4	○5

Part III - d

請排序你購買服飾時，給予服裝意見最重要的三個人。(1為最重要, 接著為2及3)

母親 / 父親　　兄弟 / 姊妹　　老公 / 老婆　　朋友　　男女朋友

同學　　同事　　售貨員　　其他　　(請寫出來)

Part III - e

請閱讀下列文句，並直接圈選你認同的答案

1. 你家人支持你購買服飾的行為嗎?

○1.完全不贊成　　○2.不贊成　　○3.適中　　○4.贊成　　○5.完全贊成

2. 你的朋友(包含男女朋友)支持你購買服飾的行為嗎?

○1.完全不贊成　　○2.不贊成　　○3.適中　　○4.贊成　　○5.完全贊成

3. 售貨員支持你購買服飾的行為嗎?

○1.完全不贊成　　○2.不贊成　　○3.適中　　○4.贊成　　○5.完全贊成

你認為你會接受這些人對您購買服裝的建議嗎? 請直接圈選答案

4. 你的家人會多常影響你購買服飾的決定嗎?

○1.完全沒有　　○2.很少　　○3.有時　　○4.經常　　○5.非常多

5. 你的朋友會多常影響你購買服飾的決定嗎?

○1.完全沒有　　○2.很少　　○3.有時　　○4.經常　　○5.非常多

6. 售貨員多會常影響你購買服飾的決定嗎

○1.完全沒有　　○2.很少　　○3.有時　　○4.經常　　○5.非常多

確定送出　　重新填寫

消費者的基本資料

1. 請問您是　○男性　　　○女性

2. 請問您是　　○大學生　　○研究生

3. 請問您的居住地？○北部　○中部　　○南部

4. 請問您有在工作嗎?　○沒有　○有

　　如果有的話, 請問是 □打工性質　– 您的工作是

　　　　　　　　　□全職的工作 – 您的工作是

5. 請問您的年齡層介於

　　○18-24　　○25-31　　○32-38　　○39-45　　○46-
　　　　　　　52　　○53-59　　○60+

6. 請問你家庭的年收入所得為多少？

　　○少於50萬　　　　　　　　○51萬～70
萬　　　　　　　　○71萬～90萬

　　○91萬～110萬　　　　　　○111萬～130
萬　　　　　　　　○131萬～150 萬

　　○151萬~170萬　　　　　　○171萬~ 190
萬　　　　　　　　○191萬以上

謝謝您撥空時間來填寫這份問卷，若有任何問題或是對這份問卷有任何建議麻煩您告知

確定送出　　重新填寫

Appendix F. Human Subjects Approval Memo

Florida State
UNIVERSITY

Office of the Vice President For Research
Human Subjects Committee
Tallahassee, Florida 32306-2763
(850) 644-8673 · FAX (850) 644-4392

APPROVAL MEMORANDUM

Date: 4/22/2004

To:
Yun Wang
MC 1492

Dept.: **TEXTILES AND CONSUMER SCIENCES**

From: **John Tomkowiak , Chair**

Re: **Use of Human Subjects in Research**
Roles of Consumers' affects, attitude, social factors and individual difference in apparel purchase intention and behavior in two cultures.

The forms that you submitted to this office in regard to the use of human subjects in the proposal referenced above have been reviewed by the Secretary, the Chair, and two members of the Human Subjects Committee. Your project is determined to be Exempt per 45 CFR § 46.101(b) 2 and has been approved by an accelerated review process.

The Human Subjects Committee has not evaluated your proposal for scientific merit, except to weigh the risk to the human participants and the aspects of the proposal related to potential risk and benefit. This approval does not replace any departmental or other approvals, which may be required.

If the project has not been completed by **4/21/2005** you must request renewed approval for continuation of the project.

You are advised that any change in protocol in this project must be approved by resubmission of the project to the Committee for approval. Also, the principal investigator must promptly report, in writing, any unexpected problems causing risks to research subjects or others.

By copy of this memorandum, the chairman of your department and/or your major professor is reminded that he/she is responsible for being informed concerning research projects involving human subjects in the department, and should review protocols of such investigations as often as needed to insure that the project is being conducted in compliance with our institution and with DHHS regulations.

This institution has an Assurance on file with the Office for Protection from Research Risks. The Assurance Number is IRB00000446.

Cc: Dr. Jeanne Heitmeyer
HSC No. 2004.286

References

Aaker, D. A., Stayman, D. M., & Vezina, R. (1988). Identifying feeling elicited by advertising. *Psychology and Marketing, 5* (1), 1-16.

Aiken, L. S., & West, S. G. (1991). *Multiple regression: Testing and interpreting interaction.* Newbury Park: Sage.

Ajzen, I. (1985). From intentions to actions: A theory of planned behavior. In J. Kuhland & J. Beckman (Eds.), *Action-control: From cognitions to behavior* (pp. 11-39). Heidelberg: Springer.

Ajzen, I., & Fishbein, M. (1980). *Understanding attitudes and predicting social behavior.* Englewood Cliff, NJ: Prentice Hall.

Ajzen, I., & Madden, T. J. (1986). Prediction of goal-directed behavior: Attitudes, intentions, and perceived behavioral control. *Journal of Experimental Social Psychology, 22,* 453-474.

Akhter, S., Andrews, J. C., and Durvasula, S. (1994). The influence of retail store environment on brand related judgments. *Journal of Retailing and Consumer Services, 1,* 67-76.

Al-Khaldi, M. & Wallace, R. S. O.(1999). The influence of attitudes on personal computer utilization among knowledge workers: The case of Saudi Arabia. *Information and Management.* 36(4). 185-204.

Alpert, J. I. & Alpert, M. I. (1990). Music influences on mood and purchase intentions. *Psychology & Marketing, 7,* 109-133.

Arndt, J. (1972). Intrafamilial homogeneity for perceived risk and opinion leadership. *Journal of Advertising, 1,* 40-47.

Babbie, E. (2001). *The practice of social research* (9th ed.). Belmont, CA: Wadsworth.

Bagozzi, R. P., & Warshaw, P. R. (1990). Trying to consume. *Journal of Consumer Research, 17,* 127-140.

Baker, J. (1986). The role of environment in marketing services: The consumer perspective. In J. A. Cepeil et al. (Eds.), *The services challenge: Integrating for competitive advantage* (pp. 79-84). Chicago, IL: American Marking Association.

Baker, J., Levy, M., & Grewal, D. (1992). An experimental approach to making retail store environmental decisions. *Journal of Retailing, 68,* 445-460.

Baron, R. M., & Kenny, D. A. (1986). The moderator- mediator variable distinction in social psychological research: Conceptual, strategic, and statistical considerations. *Journal of Personality and Social Psychology,* 51, 1173-1182.

Batson, C. D., Shaw, L. L., & Oleson, K. C. (1992). Differentiating affect, emotion and mood: Toward functionally based conceptual definitions. In M.S. Clark (Ed.), *Review of Personality and Social Psychology* (Vol.13, pp. 294-326). Newbury Park, CA: Sage Publications.

Bearden, W. O., & Etzel, M. J. (1982). Reference group influence on product and brand purchase decisions. *Journal of Consumer Research, 9*, 183-194.

Bearden, W. O., & Netemeyer, R. G. (1999). *Handbook of marketing scales: Multi-item measures for marketing and consumer behavior research.* Thousand Oaks, CA: Sage Publications.

Bellenger, D. N., & Korgaonkar, P. K. (1980). Profiling the recreational shopper. *Journal of Retailing, 56,* 77-82.

Blackwell, R. D., Miniard, P. W., & Engel, J. F.(2001). *Consumer behavior.* New York, Harcourt College Publishers.

Bloch, P. H., Ridgway, N. M., & Dawson, S. A. (1994). The shopping mall as consumer habitat. *Journal of Retailing, 70,* 23-42.

BMDP Statistical Software, Inc. (1993), *BMDP Statistical Software Manual, Release 7,* Vols. 1 and 2, Los Angeles: BMDP Statistical Software.

Bond, M. H., Leung, K., & Wan, K. C. (1982). How does cultural collectivism operate? *Journal of Cross-Cultural Psychology, 13,* 186-200.

Booth Davies, J. (1992). *The myth of addiction: An application of the psychological Theory of Attribution to illicit drug use.* Switzerland: Harwood Academic Publishers.

Breckler, S. J., & Wiggins, E. C. (1989). Affect versus evaluation in the structure of attitudes. *Journal of Experimental Social Psychology, 25*, 253-271.

Briley, D. A., & Wyer, R. S. (2001). Transitory determinants of values and decisions: The utility (or nonutility) of individualism and collectivism in understanding cultural differences. *Social Cognition, 19,* 197-227.

Briley, D. A., & Wyer, R. S. (2002). The effects of group membership salience on the avoidance of negative outcomes: Implications for social and consumer decisions. *Journal of Consumer Research, 29,* 400-415.

Browne, B., & Kaldenberg, D. (1997). Conceptualizing self-monitoring: Links to materialism and product involvement. *Journal of Consumer Marketing, 14,* 31-44.

Bruner II, G. C., & Hensel, P. J. (1996). *Marketing scales handbook.* Chicago: American Marketing Association.

Cacioppo, J. T., & Petty, R. E. (1982). The need for cognition. *Journal of Personality and Social Psychology, 42,* 116-131.

Cacioppo, J. T., Petty, R. E., & Chuan, K. F. (1984). The efficient assessment of need for cognition. *Journal of Personality Assessment, 48,* 306-307.

Calder, J., Phillips, L. W, & Tybout, A. (1981). "Designing research for application," *Journal of Consumer Research*, 8, 197-207.

Callow, M. A., & Schiffman, L. G. (2002). Over-reading into the visual print ad: The development of weak implicatures among consumers from the United States, Spain, and the Philippines [Abstract]. *Advance in Consumer Research, 29,* 49.

Carlson, E. R. (1956). Attitude change through modification of attitude structure. *Journal of abnormal and Social Psychology, 52,* 256-261.

Carlson, A. W., Laczniak, R. N., & Grossbart, S. (1994). Family communication patterns and marketplace motivations, attitudes, and behaviors of children and mothers. *Journal of Consumer Affairs, 28*, 25-53.

Casselman, M. A., & Damhorst, M. L. (1991). Behavioral intentions and the apparel purchase decision: Testing the Fishbein Model. *International Textile and Apparel Association Proceedings, 48,* 77.

Cassill, N. L., & Drake, M. F. (1987). Apparel selection criteria related to female consumers' lifestyle. *Clothing and Textiles Research Journal, 6*(1), 20-28.

Chan, R. Y., & Lau, L. (1998). A test of the Fishbein-Ajzen Behavioral Intentions Model under Chinese cultural settings: Are there any differences between PRC and Hong Kong consumers? *Journal of Marketing Practice: Applied Marketing Science, 4*(3), 85-101.

Chang, Y., Burns, L. D., & Noel, C. J. (1996). Attitudinal versus normative influence in the purchase of brand-name causal apparel. *Family and Consumer Sciences Research Journal, 25*(1), 79-109.

Childers, T. L., & Rao, A. R. (1992). The influence of familial and peer-based reference groups on consumer decisions. *Journal of Consumer Research, 19*, 198-211.

Clarke, K., & Belk, R. W. (1978). The effects of product involvement and task definition on anticipated consumer effort. *Advances in Consumer Research, 5*, 313-318.

Cohen, J. B., & Areni, C. S. (1991). Affect and consumer behavior. In T. S. Robertson & H. H. Kassarjian (Eds.), *Handbook of consumer behavior* (pp. 188-240). Englewood Cliffs, NJ: Prentice-Hall.

Cohen, J., & Cohen, P. (1983). *Applied multiple regressional/correlation analysis for the behavioral sciences.* Hillsdale, NJ: Erlbaum.

Cote, J. A., & Tansuhaj, P.S. (1989). Culture bound assumptions in behavior intention models. *Advances in Consumer Research, 16*, 105-109.

Crowley, A. E. (1993). The two dimensional impact of color on shopping. *Marketing letters, 4*, 59-69.

Davidson, A. R., & Thompson, E. (1980). Cross-cultural studies of attitudes and beliefs. In H. C. Triandis (Ed.), *The handbook of cross-cultural psychology, 5*, 25-71.

Davis, L. L. (1987). Consumer use of label information in ratings of clothing quality and clothing fashionability. *Clothing of Textiles and Research Journal, 6* (1), 8-14.

DeLong, M. R., & Minshall, B., & Larntz, K. (1987). Predicting consumer response to fashion apparel. *Home Economics Research Journal, 16*(2), 150-160.

Derbaix, C., & Pham, M. T. (1998). For the development of measure of emotion in marketing: Summary of prerequisites. In M. Lambkin, G. Foxall, F. A. Raaij, & B. Heilbrunn (Eds.), *European perspectives on consumer behaviour* (pp.140-155). London: Prentice Hall Europe.

Dollinger, S. J., & DiLalla, D. L. (1996). "Cleaning Up Data And Running Preliminary Analyses," in: F. T. L. Leong and J. T. Austin, Eds. *The Psychology Research Handbook*, Thousand Oaks, CA: Sage Publications, pp. 167-176.

Donovan, R., & Rossiter, J. (1982). Store atmosphere: An environmental psychology approach. *Journal of Retailing, 58,* 34-57.

Donovan, R., Rossiter, J., Marcoolyn, G., & Newdale, A. (1994). Store atmosphere and purchasing behavior. *Journal of Retailing, 70*, 283-294.

Dube, L., Chebat, J. C., & Morin, S. (1995). The effects of background music on consumers' desire to affiliate in buyer-seller interactions. *Psychology and Marketing, 12,* 305-319.

Eagly, A. A., & Chaiken, S. (1993). *The psychology of attitudes.* Fort Worth, TX: Harcourt Brace Jovanovich.

Eckman, M., Damhorst, M. L., & Kadolph, S. J. (1990). Toward a model of the in-store purchase decision process: Consumer use of criteria for evaluating women's apparel. *Clothing and Textiles Research Journal, 8*(2), 13-22.

Edell, J. A., & Burke, M. C. (1987). The power of feelings in understanding advertising effects. *Journal of Consumer Research, 14*, 421-433.

Edwards, S., & Shackley, M. (1992). Measuring the effectiveness of retail window display as an element of the marketing mix. *International Journal of Advertising, 11,* 193-202.

Engel, J. F., Blackwell, R. D., & Miniard, P. W. (1995). *Consumer behavior* (8th ed.). Chicago: Dryden Press.

Epstein, S., Pacini, R., Denes-Raj, V., & Heier, H. (1996). Individual differences in intuitive-experiential and analytical-rational thinking styles. *Journal of Personality and Social Psychology, 71*(2), 390-405.

Eroglu, S. A., & Machleit, K. A. (1990). An empirical examination of retail crowding: Antecedents and consequences. *Journal of Retailing, 66,* 201-221.

Evans, F. R., Christiansen, T., & Gill, J.D. (1996). The impact of social influence and role expectations on shopping center patronage intentions. *Journal of the Academy of Marketing Science, 24*(3), 208-218.

Evrard, Y., & Aurier, P. (1996). Identification and validation of the components of person-object relationship. *Journal of Business Research, 37*, 127-134.

Fairhurst, A., Good, L., & Gentry, J. (1989). Fashion involvement: An instrument validation procedure. *Clothing and Textile Research Journal, 7(3)*, 10-14.

Festinger, L. A. (1957). *Theory of cognitive dissonance.* Evanston, IL: Row, Peterson.

Festinger, R. A., Sheffler, B., & Meoli, J. (1989). There's something social happening at the mall. *Journal of Business and Psychology, 4*, 49-63.

Fishbein, M. (1963). An investigation of the relationship between beliefs about an object and the attitude toward that object. *Human Relations,* 233-240.

Fiske, S. T., & Taylor, S. E (1991). *Social cognition.* NY: McGraw-Hill, Inc. (pp. 410-461).

Flynn, L., & Goldsmith, R. (1993). A causal model of consumer involvement: Replication and critique. *Journal of Social Behavior and Personality, 8* (6), 129-142.

Fong, C. P. S. & Wyer, R. S. (2003). Cultural, social, and emotional determinants of decisions under uncertainty. *Organizational Behavioral and Human Decision Processes, 90,* 304-322.

Freedman, R. (1986). *Beauty bound.* Lexington, MA: Lexington Books.

Gagnon, J. P., and Osterhaus, J. T. (1985). Research note: Effectiveness of floor displays on the sales of retail products. *Journal of Retailing, 61,* 104-116.

Gardner, M. P. (1985). Does attitude toward the ad affect brand attitude under a brand evaluation set? *Journal of Marketing Research, 22,* 281-300.

Ger, G. (1989). Nature of effects of affect on judgment: Theoretical and methodological issues. In P. Cafferata and A. M. Tybout, (Eds.), *Cognitive and Affective Responses to Advertising* (pp. 21-30). Lexington, MA: Lexington Books.

Gergen, K. & Gergen M. (1981). *Social Psychology.* NY: Harcourt Brace Jovanovich.

Goldsmith, R., Moore, M., Beaudoin, P. (1999). Fashion innovativeness and self-concept: A replication. *Journal of Product and Brand management, 8*(1), 7-18.

Hair, J. F., Anderson, R. E., Tatham, R. L., & Black, W. C. (1998). *Multivariate data analysis.* Upper Saddle River, NJ: Prentice-Hall.

Harold, H. K. (1965). Two functions of reference groups. In P. Harold & B. Siedenberg (Eds.), *Basic studies in social psychology,* (pp. 210-214). NY: Holt, Rinehart and Winston.

Härtel, C., McColl-Kennedy, J., & McDonald, L. (1998). Incorporating attributional theory and the theory of reasoned action within an affective events theory framework to produce a contingency predictive model of consumer reactions to organizational mishaps. In J. W. Alba & W. Hutchinson (Eds.), *Advances in Consumer Research: Vol. 25.* (pp. 428-432). Provo, UT: Association for Consumer Research.

Haugtvedt, C., Petty, R. E., Cacioppo, J. T., & Steidley, T. (1988). Personality and Ad effectiveness: Exploring the utility of need for cognition. In Michael J. H. (Ed.), *Advance in Consumer Research* (Vol. 15, pp. 209-212). Provo, UT: Association for Consumer Research.

Havlena, W. J., & Holbrook, M. B. (1986). The varieties of consumption experience: Comparing two types of typologies of emotion in consumer behavior. *Journal of Consumer Research, 13,* 394-404.

Heckler, S. E., & Childers, T. L., & Arunachalam, R. (1989). Intergenerational influences in adult buying behaviors: An examination of moderating factors. In T. K. Srull (Ed.), *Advances in Consumer Research, 16,* (pp. 276-284). Provo, UT: Association for Consumer Research.

Heider, F. (1946). Attitudes and cognitive organizations. *Journal of Psychology, 21,* 107-112.

Heitmeyer, J., & Kind, K. (2004). Retailing in my backyard: Consumer perceptions of retail establishments located within new urbanist communities. *Journal of Shopping Center Research, 11,* 33-53.

Herr, P. M. (1995). Whither fact, artifact and attitude: Reflections on the theory of reasoned action. *Journal of Consumer Psychology, 4,* 371-380.

Hilgard, E. R. (1980). The trilogy of mind: Cognition, affection, and conation. *Journal of the History of the Behavioral Sciences, 16(2),* 107-117.

Hofstede, G. (2001). *Culture's consequences: Comparing values, behaviors, institutions, and organizations across nations.* Beverley Hill, CA: Sage Press.

Hoffman, A. M. (1970). *The daily needs and interests of older people.* Springfield, IL: Charles C. Thomas.

Holbrook, M. B., & Batra, R. (1987). Assessing the role of emotions as mediators of consumer response to advertising. *Journal of Consumer Research, 14,* 404-420.

Hong, J. W., Muderrisoglu, A., & Zinkhan, G. M. (1987). Cultural differences and advertising expression: A comparative content analysis of Japanese and US magazine advertising. *Journal of Advertising, 16*(1), 55-63.

Hsiao, C. F. (1993). *Taiwanese and U.S. students in a U.S. university: Evaluative criteria for purchasing leisurewear.* Unpublished master's thesis, University of Missouri, Columbia.

Hsu, H-J., & Burns, L. D. (2002). Clothing evaluative criteria: A cross-national comparison of Taiwanese and United States consumers. *Clothing and Textiles Research Journal, 20,* 246-252.

Inman, J. J., McAlister, L., & Hoyer, W. D. (1990). Promotion signal: Proxy for a price cut. *Journal of Consumer Research, 17,* 74-81.

Isen, A. M. (1989). Some ways in which affect influences cognitive processes: Implication for advertising and consumer behavior. In P. Cafferata and A. M. Tybout, (Eds.), *Cognitive and affective responses to advertising* (pp. 91-117). Lexington, MA: Lexington Books.

Isen, A. M., Clark, M., & Schwartz, M. F. (1976). Duration of the effect of good mood on helping: Footprints on the sands of time. *Journal of Personality and Social Psychology, 34* (3), 385-393.

Iyer, E. S. (1989). Unplanned purchasing: Knowledge of shopping environment and time pressure. *Journal of Retailing, 65,* 40-57.

Izard, C. E. (1972). *Patterns of emotions: A new analysis of anxiety and depression.* New York: Academic Press.

Izard, C. E. (1977). *Human emotions.* New York: Plenum Press.

Jenkins, M. C. (1973). *Clothing and textile evaluative criteria: Basis for benefit segmentation and reflection of underlying values.* Dissertation Abstracts International 34(11), 5547B. (University Microfilms No. AAC74-10977).

Karahanna, E., Straub, D. W. (1999). The psychological origins of perceived usefulness and ease-of-use. *Information & Management, 35,* 237-250.

Kardes, F. R. (2001). *Consumer behavior and managerial decision making* (2nd ed.). Upper Saddle River, NJ: Prentice Hall.

Kemper, T. (1987). How many emotions are there? Wedding the social and the autonomic components. *American Journal of Sociology, 93,* 263-289.

Kim, H. S. (2000). Examination of emotional response to apparel brand advertisements. *Journal of Fashion Marketing and Management, 4* (4), 303-313.

Krugman, H. (1965). The impact of television in advertising: Learning without involvement. *Public Opinion Quarterly, 29,* 349-356.

Lastovicka, J. L., & Gardner, D. M. (1978). Components of involvement. In J. C. Maloney & B. Silverman (Eds.), *Attitude research plays for high stakes* (pp. 53-73). Chicago: American Marketing Association.

Lam, T., Pine, R., & Baum, T. (2003). Subjective norms: Effects on job satisfaction. *Annals of Tourism Research, 30,* 160-177.

Lazarus, R. S. (1991). Progress on a cognitive-motivational-relational theory of emotion. *American Psychologist, 46,* 819-834.

Lazarus, R. S., & Smith, C. A. (1988). Knowledge and appraisal in the cognition-emotion relationship. *Cognition and Emotion, 2,* 281-300.

Lee, M., & Burn, L. D. (1993). Self-consciousness and clothing purchase criteria of Korean and United States college women. *Clothing and Textiles Research Journal, 11,* 32-40.

Lee, C., & Green, R. T. (1990). Cross-cultural examination of the Fishbein behavioral intentions model. *Journal of International Business Studies, 22*(2), 289-305.

Loudon, D. L., & Della Bitta, A. J. (1993). *Consumer behavior: Concepts and applications* (4th ed.). New York: McGraw-Hill.

Lutz, R. J. (1990). The role of attitude theory in marketing. In H. H. Kassarjian & T. S. Robertson (Eds.), *Perspectives in Consumer Behavior* (4th ed., pp. 317-319). Upper Saddle River, NJ: Prentice Hall.

Machleit, K. A., & Eroglu, S. A. (2000). Describing and measuring emotional response to shopping experience. *Journal of Business Research, 49,* 101-111.

Madden, T. J., Ellen, P. S., & Ajzen, I. (1992). A comparison of the Theory of Planned Behavior and the Theory of Reasoned Action. *Personality and Social Psychology Bulletin, 18,* 3-9.

Malhotra, N. K., & McCort, J. D. (2001). A cross-cultural comparison of behavioral intention models: Theoretical consideration and an empirical investigation. *International Marketing Review, 18*(3), 235-269.

Martin, C. (1998). Relationship marketing: A high-involvement product attribute approach. *Journal of Product and Brand Management, 7,* 6-26.

Mathieson, K. (1991). Predicting user intentions: Comparing the technology acceptance model with the theory of planned behavior. *Information Systems Research, 2,* 173-191.

McGoldrick, P. J., & Thompson, M. G. (1992). Regional shopping centers: Out-of-town vs. in-town. Aldershopt: Avebury.

McLean, F. P., Roper, L. L., & Smothers, R. (1986). Imported versus domestic blouses: Women's preference and purchase motives. *Home Economics Research Journal, 14*(3), 306-313.

Mehrabian, A., & Russell, J. A. (1974). *An approach to environmental psychology.* Cambridge, MA: MIT press.

Miniard, P. W., & Barone, M. J. (1997). The case for noncognitive determinants of attitude: A critique of Fishbein and Middlestadt. *Journal of Consumer Psychology, 6,* 39-44.

Mitchell, A. A., & Olson, J. C. (1981). Are product attribute beliefs the only mediator of advertising effects on brand attitude? *Journal of Marketing Research, 18,* 318-332.

Mittal, B. (1995). A comparative analysis of four scales of consumer involvement. *Psychology & Marketing, 12(7),* 663-682.

Moore, T. S. (1990). A study of pharmacist and consumer attitudes and intentions regarding the selection of generic prescription drug products and the effect of situational variables (drugs). *Dissertation Abstracts International, 51* (06), 2840B. (UMI No. 9031668).

Morris, J. D., Woo, C., Geason, J. A., & Kim, J. (2002). The power of affect: Predicting intention. *Journal of Advertising Research, 3,* 7-17.

Oliver, R. L. (1994). Conceptual issues in the structural analysis of consumption emotion, satisfaction, and quality. In Chris. T. Allen and Deborah R. J. (Eds.), *Advances in Consumer Research, Vol. 21,* (pp. 16-22). Provo, UT: Association for Consumer Research.

Oliver, R. L. (1997). *Satisfaction- A Behavioral Perspective on the Consumer.* Irwin/McGraw-Hill.

Oliver, R. L., & Bearden, W. O. (1985). Crossover effects in the theory of reasoned action: A moderating influence attempt. *Journal of Consumer Research, 12,* 324-340.

Onkvisit, S., & Shaw, J. J. (1994). *Consumer behavior: Strategy and analysis.* New York: Macmillan College.

Ortony, A., & Turner, T. J. (1990). What's basic about basic emotions? *Psychological Review, 97,* 315-331.

Panksepp, J. (1982). Toward a general psychobiological theory of emotions. *The Behavioral and Brain Science, 11,* 341-364.

Pao, W. T. (1996). *New topics for the new generations.* Taipei: Hei Dai publish.

Park C. W. & Lessig, V. P. (1977). Students and housewives: Differences in susceptibility to reference group influence. *Journal of Consumer Research, 4,* 102-110.

Patton, W. E. (1981). Quantity of information and information display type as a predictor of consumer choice of product brands. *Journal of Consumer Affairs, 15,* 92-105.

Peak, H. (1955). Attitude and motivation. In M. R. Jones (Ed.), *Nebraska Symposium on Motivation* (Vol.3, pp.149-188). Lincoln: University of Nebraska Press.

Petty, R. E., & Cacioppo, J. T. (1986). *Communication and persuasion: Central and peripheral routes to attitude change.* New York: Springer/ Verlag.

Plutchik, R. (1980). *Emotion: A psycho evolutionary synthesis.* New York: Harper and Row Press.

Plutchik, R. (1989). Measuring emotions and their derivatives. In R. Plutchik & H. Kellerman (Eds.), *Emotion: Theory, research and experience, 4,* 1-36.

Raman, N. V., Chattopadhyay, P., & Hoyer, W. D. (1995). Do consumers seek emotional situations: The need for emotion scale. In F. Kardes and M. Sujan (Eds.), *Advances in Consumer Research (Vol. 22,* pp. 537-542). Provo, UT: Association for Consumer Research.

Richins, M. L. (1987). Media, materialism, and human happiness. In M. Wallendorf and P. Anderson (Eds.), *Advances in Consumer Research* (Vol. 14, pp. 352-356). Provo, UT: Association for Consumer Research.

Richins, M. L. (1997). Measuring emotions in the consumption experience. *Journal of Consumer Research, 24,* 127-146.

Roseman, I. J., Spindel, M. S., & Jose, P. E. (1990). Appraisals of emotion-eliciting events: Testing a theory of discrete emotions. *Journal of Personality and Social Psychology, 59,* 899-915.

Rosenberg, M. J. (1956). Cognitive structure and attitudinal affect. *Journal of Abnormal and Social Psychology, 53,* 367-372.

Rosenberg, M. J., & Hovland, L. (1960). *Attitude organization and change: An analysis of consistency among attitude component.* New Haven: Yale University.

Schiffman, L., & Kanuk, L. L. (2004). *Consumer behavior* (8th ed.). Upper Saddle River, NJ: Prentice Hall.

Schwarz, N., & Clore, G. L. (1988). How do I feel about it? The informative function of affective states. In K. Fiedler & J. Forgas (Eds.), *Affect, cognition, and social Behavior* (pp. 44-62). Toronto: Hogrefe.

Sears, D. O. (1983). The persistence of early political predispositions. In L. Wheeler & R. Shaver (Eds.), *Review of personality and social psychology* (pp. 79-116). Beverly Hills, CA: Sage Publications.

Shaver, P. R., Wu, S., & Schwartz, J. C. (1992). Cross-cultural similarities and differences in emotion and its representation. In M. S. Clark (Ed.), *Review of Personality and Social Psychology* (Vol.13, pp. 175-212). Newbury Park, CA: Sage Publications.

Shen, D., Dickson, M. A., Lennon, S., Montalto, C., & Zhang, L. (2003). Cultural influences on Chinese consumers' intentions to purchase apparel: Test and extension of the Fishbein Behavioral Intentional Model. *Clothing and Textiles Research Journal, 21*(2), 89-99.

Sheppard, B. H., Hartwick, J., & Warshaw, P. R. (1988). The Theory of Reasoned Action: A meta-analysis of past research with recommendations for modifications and future research. *Journal of Consumer Research, 15,* 325-343.

Sheth, J. (1982). Some comments on Triandis: The model of choice behavior in marketing. In Sheth, J. (Ed.), *Research in Marketing, Vol. 6,* (Suppl. 1, pp.145-162). Greenwich, CT: JAI Press.

Shim, S., & Drake, M. F. (1990). Consumer intention to utilize electronic shopping: The Fishbein behavioral intentional model. *Journal of Direct Marketing, 4*(3), 22-33.

Shimp, T. A., & Sharma, S. (1987). Consumer ethnocentrism: Construction and validation of the CETSCALE. *Journal of Marketing Research, 24,* 280-289.

Sillars, A. L. (1995). Communication and family culture. In M. A. Fitzpatrick & A. L. Vangelisti (Eds.), *Explaining family interactions* (pp. 375-399). Thousand Oaks, CA: Sage Publications.

Smith, C. A., Haynes, K. N., Lazarus, R. S., & Pope, L. K. (1993). In search of the "Hot" cognitions: Attributions, appraisals, and their relation to emotion. *Journal of Personality and Social Psychology, 65,* 916-929.

Smith, C. A., & Lazarus, R. S. (1990). Emotion and adaptation. In L. A. Pervin (Ed.), *Handbook of personality: Theory and research* (pp. 609-637). New York: Guilford Press.

Smith, P., & Burns, D. J. (1996). Atmospherics and retail environments: The case of the "power aisle." *International Journal of Retail and Distribution Management, 24,* 7-14.

Smucker, B., & Creekmore, A. M. (1972). Adolescents' clothing conformity: Awareness and peer acceptance. *Home Economics Research Journal, 1,* 92-97.

Solomon, M. R. (1983). The role of products as social stimuli: A symbolic interactionism perspective. *Journal of Consumer Research, 10,* 319-329.

Solomon, M., & Schopler, J. (1982). Self-consciousness and clothing. *Personality and Social Psychology Bulletin, 8,* 508-514.

Spangenberg, E. R., Crowley, A. E., and Henderson, P. W. (1996). Improving the store environment: Do olfactory cues affect evaluations and behaviors? *Journal of Marketing, 60,* 67-80.

Statistical Yearbook of the Republic of China (2003). ISSN No. 0256-7857. Republic of China, Taipei, Directorate-General of Budget, Accounting and Statistics Executive Yuan.

Sunil, E. (1998). The role of affect in marketing. *Journal of Business Research, 42,* 190-215.

Trafimow, D., & Fishbein, M. (1994). The moderating effect of behavior type on the subjective norm-behavior relationship. *The Journal of Social Psychology, 134,* 755-759.

Tigert, D., Ring, L., & King, C. (1976). Fashion involvement and buying behavior: A methodological study. *Advance in Consumer Research, 3,* 46-52.

Tigert, D., King, C., & Ring, L. (1980). Fashion involvement: A cross cultural analysis. *Advance in Consumer Research, 7,* 17-21.

Triandis, H. C. (1977). *Interpersonal behavior.* Monterey, CA: Brooks/Cole Publishing.

Triandis, H. C. (1982). A model of choice in marketing. In Sheth, J. (Ed.), *Research in Marketing, Vol. 6* (Suppl. 1, pp.145-162). Greenwich, CT: JAI Press.

Triandis, H. C. (1989). The self and social behavior in differing cultural contexts. *Psychological Review, 96,* 506-520.

Triandis, H. C. (1995). *Individualism and collectivism.* Boulder, CO: Westview.

Turley, L. W., & Milliman, R. E. (2000). Atmospheric effects on shopping behavior: A review of the experimental evidence. *Journal of Business Research, 49,* 193-211.

United States Department of Commerce (2001). U.S. foreign trade highlights. Retrieved February 12, 2003, from http://www.ita.doc.gov/td/industry/otea/usfth.

Vijayasarathy, L.R., & Jones, J.M. (2000). Intentions to shop using Internet catalogues: Exploring the effects of product types, shopping orientations, and attitudes toward computer. *Electronic Markets, 10 (1),* 29-38.

Wakefield, K. L., & Baker, J. (1998). Excitement at the Mall: Determinants and effects on shopping response. *Journal of Retailing, 74,* 515-539.

Wakefield, K. L., & Blodgett, J. G. (1996). The effect of the servicescape on customers' behavioral intentions in leisure service settings. *Journal of Services Marketing, 10(6),* 43-59.

Wang, Y. (2005). The Y generation's consumption of the generic brands apparels in Taiwan and the quality of these apparels. *Proceedings of the International Textile and Apparel Association,* Alexandria, VA, USA.

Wang, Y., & Heitmeyer, J. (2006). Consumer attitude toward US versus domestic apparel in Taiwan. *International Journal of Consumer Studies, 30(1),* 64-74.

Ward, J. C., Bitner, M. J., & Barnes, J. (1992). Measuring the prototypicality and meaning of retail environments. *Journal of Retailing, 68,* 194-200.

Weiner, B. (1985). An Attributional theory of achievement motivation and emotion. *Psychological Review, 92,* 548-573.

Weiner, B. (1995). *Judgments of responsibility.* NY: The Guilford Press.

Weiss, H., M. & Cropanzano, R. (1996). Affective events theory: A theoretical discussion of the structure, causes and consequences of affective experiences at work. *Research in Organizational Behavior, 18,* 1-74.

Wilkinson, J. B., Mason, J. B., and Paksoy, C. H. (1982). Assessing the impact of short-term supermarket strategy variables. *Journal of Marketing Research, 14.* 72-86.

Woodson, L. G., Childers, T. L., & Winn, P. R. (1976). Intergenerational influences in the purchase of auto insurance. In W. B. Locander (Ed.), *Marketing looking outward: 1976 Business Proceedings* (pp. 43-49). Chicago: American Marketing Association.

Workman, J. E. (1990). Effects of fiber content labeling on perception of apparel characteristics. *Clothing and Textile Research Journal, 8*(3), 19-24.

Wright, P. (1974). Analyzing media effects on advertising response. *Public Opinion Quarterly, 38,* 192-205.

Yang, K. (1992). Do traditional and modern values coexist in a modern Chinese society? (in Chinese) Proceedings of the Chinese Perspectives on Values, Taiwan, 117-158.

Yi, Y. (1990). Cognitive and affective priming effects of the context for print advertisements. *Journal of Advertising, 19* (2), 40-48.

Young, H. M., Lierman, L. Powell-Cope, G., Kasprzyk, D., & Benoliel, J. Q. (1991). Operationalizing the Theory of Planned Behavior. *Research in Nursing and Health, 14,* 137-144.

Zaichkowsky, J. (1985). Measuring the involvement construct. *Journal of Consumer Research, 12,* 341-352.

Biographical Sketch

Yun Wang was born in Taiwan, on September, 17, 1972. She began to study fashion design at the age of fifteen in Tainan Junior College of Home Economics. After graduation she transferred to Columbia College in Missouri, studying business, and, subsequently, received her Bachelor of Arts degree in 1994, December. She applied to a few graduate schools before she went back to her country. However, without the support from an assistantship or fellowship, she decided to work for awhile and save some money. She worked at a Textile and Apparel International Buying Office in Taipei, Taiwan. While she was working at the buying office, the College of Human Sciences in Florida State University sent her a letter to congratulate her on being accepted for admission to graduate school with the fellowship. Yun resigned her job and came to the U.S. in August, 1995. To further her interest in fashion merchandising, after she graduated in mater degree she worked as sales manager at Burdines department store in Florida. After she went back to Taiwan she got a Marketing Manager Job for prestige brand- Salvantore Ferragamo. Later on, she started to teach in Shih-Chien University and decided "teaching" is really what she like to do in future. She returned to FSU in 2002 to pursue her PH.D. and plan to graduate in Spring, 2006.

She has received numerous awards and honors including the 2003-2004 Lois Dickey Fellowship and the 2002-2003 Marjorie Joseph Scholarship, both of these honors were awarded by the International Textile and Apparel Association. She has been inducted into the Hortense Glenn and Kappa Omicron Nu honor societies at Florida State University and received the Thomas M. & Eileen Rhodes Culligan Scholarship from the Department of Textiles and Consumer Sciences in 2003.

She has a tremendous amount of initiative and competency, is an extremely responsible and conscientious individual who can accomplish the tasks before her in a most appropriate manner. She is a bright, hardworking, energetic, generous and kind individual. She not only has teaching and research experience but also has extensive industry experience as a marketing planner, sales manager, fabric buyer, and apparel broker.

實踐大學數位出版合作系列
社會科學類　AF0060

A Cross-Cultural Study of Consumer Attitudes and Emotional Responses of Apparel Purchase Behavior

作　　者	王韻（Yun Wang）
統籌策劃	葉立誠
文字編輯	王雯珊
視覺設計	賴怡勳
執行編輯	詹靚秋
圖文排版	黃莉珊
數位轉譯	徐真玉　沈裕閔
圖書銷售	林怡君
網路服務	徐國晉
法律顧問	毛國樑律師
發 行 人	宋政坤
出版印製	秀威資訊科技股份有限公司
	台北市內湖區瑞光路583巷25號1樓
	電話：(02) 2657-9211
	傳真：(02) 2657-9106
	E-mail：service@showwe.com.tw
經 銷 商	紅螞蟻圖書有限公司
	台北市內湖區舊宗路二段121巷28、32號4樓
	電話：(02) 2795-3656
	傳真：(02) 2795-4100
	http://www.e-redant.com

2007 年 5 月
BOD 一版
定價：190元

讀 者 回 函 卡

感謝您購買本書，為提升服務品質，煩請填寫以下問卷，收到您的寶貴意見後，我們會仔細收藏記錄並回贈紀念品，謝謝！

1. 您購買的書名：_____

2. 您從何得知本書的消息？

   □網路書店　□部落格　□資料庫搜尋　□書訊　□電子報　□書店

   □平面媒體　□ 朋友推薦　□網站推薦 □其他_____

3. 您對本書的評價：(請填代號　1.非常滿意 2.滿意 3.尚可 4.再改進)

   封面設計____　版面編排____　內容____　文/譯筆____　價格____

4. 讀完書後您覺得：

   □很有收獲　□有收獲　□收獲不多　□沒收獲

5. 您會推薦本書給朋友嗎？

   □會　□不會，為什麼？_____

6. 其他寶貴的意見：_____

_____

_____

_____

讀者基本資料

姓名：_____　年齡：_____　性別：□女 □男

聯絡電話：_____　E-mail：_____

地址：_____

學歷：□高中(含)以下　　□高中　□專科學校　□大學

     □研究所(含)以上 □其他_____

職業：□製造業 □金融業 □資訊業 □軍警 □傳播業 □自由業

     □服務業 □公務員 □教職　□學生 □其他_____

To：114

台北市內湖區瑞光路 583 巷 25 號 1 樓

秀威資訊科技股份有限公司　　　收

寄件人姓名：

寄件人地址：□□□

- -

(請沿線對摺寄回, 謝謝!)

秀威與 BOD

BOD（Books On Demand）是數位出版的大趨勢，秀威資訊率先運用 POD 數位印刷設備來生產書籍，並提供作者全程數位出版服務，致使書籍產銷零庫存，知識傳承不絕版，目前已開闢以下書系：

一、BOD 學術著作—專業論述的閱讀延伸
二、BOD 個人著作—分享生命的心路歷程
三、BOD 旅遊著作—個人深度旅遊文學創作
四、BOD 大陸學者—大陸專業學者學術出版
五、POD 獨家經銷—數位產製的代發行書籍

BOD 秀威網路書店：www.showwe.com.tw
政府出版品網路書店：www.govbooks.com.tw

永不絕版的故事・自己寫・永不休止的音符・自己唱